WRITING WORKSHOP SURVIVAL KIT

GARY R. MUSCHLA

THE CENTER FOR APPLIED
RESEARCH IN EDUCATION

Library of Congress Cataloging-in-Publication Data

Muschla, Gary Robert.
    Writing workshop survival kit / Gary Robert Muschla.
        p.   cm.
    Includes bibliographical references.
    ISBN 0-87628-972-3
    1. English language—Composition and exercises—Study and teaching
(Elementary)—Handbooks, manuals, etc.   2. Activity programs in education.
3. Teaching—Aids and devices.   I. Title.
    LB1576.M886   1993   92-44853
    372.6'23044—dc20   CIP

Printed in the United States of America

10   9

Many thanks to Dover Publications for
allowing us to use the illustrations.

ISBN 0-87628-972-3

**THE CENTER FOR APPLIED RESEARCH
IN EDUCATION**

On the World Wide Web at http://www.phdirect.com

Dedication

This one, too, is for Judy and Erin.

About the Author

Gary Robert Muschla received his B.A. and M.A.T. degrees from Trenton State College in New Jersey. He teaches at Appleby School in Spotswood, New Jersey, where he has developed a practical approach to the teaching of writing, conducted writing workshops for teachers and students, and edited magazines of students' writing.

In addition to his 18 years as a classroom teacher, Mr. Muschla has been a successful freelance writer, editor, and ghostwriter. He is a member of the Authors Guild, the Authors League of America, the National Writers Club, and the Associated Business Writers of America.

Mr. Muschla is also the author of two other practical resources for teachers of writing: *Writing Workshop Activities Kit: Ready-to-Use Worksheets and Enrichment Lessons for Grades 4-9* (The Center for Applied Research in Education, 1989) and *The Writing Teacher's Book of Lists* (Prentice Hall, 1991).

Acknowledgments

I'd like to thank John C. Orlick, my principal, for his continued support over the years. I'm grateful to Julia Rhodes, our district's language arts supervisor, whose love of language and writing is obvious and infectious. And I'm indebted to my colleagues who have always been helpful and encouraging.

My wife Judy deserves special thanks once again for selecting and arranging the artwork that enhances this book.

My thanks also go to Donna Cooper, my typist, who enters what is thought to be the final copy of manuscript, then patiently makes the million-and-one maddening little changes I decide on before sending it off to the publisher.

I'd also like to offer my appreciation to Sandra Hutchison, my editor, who has gone the extra mile to help me make this book what I hope is a practical and useful reference for teachers.

Finally, my thanks to my students, who, over the years, have given me far more than I have ever managed to give them.

About Writing Instruction

Effective writing is one of the most important skills a teacher can impart to his or her students. Because the ability to write well is intimately coupled with thinking, writing instruction leads to much more than the mere scribbling of words on paper. To write well, an individual must be able to focus a topic, collect and analyze information, sort through his or her thoughts, organize facts, and, finally, communicate his or her ideas to others.

Writing is a complex process, much of which goes on so deeply in the mind that even the most introspective authors have little inkling of how they do it. Yet we have learned some things about the process of writing. We know, based on the research, that all authors go through stages of prewriting, drafting, revising, editing, and publishing (or sharing), and we know that there are methods and techniques that we can share with students about the process. As students come to understand and practice the components of the writing process, they develop the skills necessary for written expression. They grow as writers.

While there are, of course, many ways to teach writing, perhaps the best is through a writing workshop, which is the focus of this resource. You'll find that the writing workshop is an exciting class to teach, for it enables you and your students to become partners in the writing experience. My best wishes to you as you begin sharing with your students the skills and techniques vital to good writing.

Gary Robert Muschla

How to Use This Resource

The *Writing Workshop Survival Kit* is divided into two major parts. Part I offers classroom management strategies and details the components of the writing process and how they fit into the writing workshop. Part II contains mini-lessons that you can implement in your writing workshop.

Part I comprises Sections 1 through 7. Sections 1 and 2 explain the writing workshop and offer specific strategies for classroom management. Sections 3 through 7 focus on the stages of the writing process and contain a variety of informative handouts and 25 specific activities for your students. All handouts are reproducible (although some teachers may prefer to make transparencies and use them with overhead projectors).

I suggest that you work through Part I first, covering the activities you regard as requisite. If your students have little experience with the writing process, you might consider doing most or all of the activities with them. However, if your students already understand the writing process, you may select the activities you believe will be most beneficial to them. Since each activity is designed to stand alone, you have much flexibility to use the ones you feel will be most helpful to your students.

Part II of the *Writing Workshop Survival Kit* contains 100 mini-lessons, divided into three sections: (1) Mini-lessons for Types of Writing, (2) Mini-lessons for the Art of Writing, and (3) Mini-lessons for the Mechanics of Writing. The mini-lessons, numbers 1 through 100, cover the different kinds of writing your students will do in your writing workshop; an author's methods, devices, and techniques; and the problems that students most often have with mechanics. Each mini-lesson stands alone and is set up in a clear, easy-to-follow format, making implementation simple. While many teachers will decide to use all the mini-lessons, others—based on the abilities of their students—may use only some. Many of the mini-lessons are accompanied by extensions, which either reinforce the focus of the lesson or offer additional information. Many of the extensions can be turned into mini-lessons of their own.

The activities and handouts of Part I together with the mini-lessons and extensions of Part II provide more than 150 separate activities/lessons you can share with your students. They will provide your students with a variety of interesting writing experiences and make your teaching in the writing workshop easier and more effective.

Table of Contents

Part One

THE WRITING PROCESS IN THE WRITING WORKSHOP

1

An Overview of the Writing Workshop

When I began teaching the writing workshop several years ago, I did not know what to expect. I was an experienced teacher of writing, I was a writer myself, and I understood and embraced the writing process. But even though I had experienced a typical workshop, had read about the writing workshop, and had gone through inservice training, I still felt uncertain. I was afraid that I was stepping into yet another one of those new ideas in education that promises great success but comes up short. After all, I felt I already had a good writing program and worried that my students would not do as well in a new one.

However, I was also drawn to the concept of the writing workshop, which provides a forum where teacher and students become *partners* in the experience of learning. I started that school year a hopeful skeptic, but soon became a believer.

You will find that the writing workshop is much more than a program designed to help children acquire the skills necessary for written language. It is a classroom in which you and your students form bonds that become the foundation of learning. In the writing workshop your teaching becomes individualized as students focus on topics that matter to them and you respond to their efforts. Because students write about their interests, worries, and dreams, the material of the writing workshop is the fabric of their lives.

The model of the writing workshop offered here (there are a number of variations available) starts with a 5- to 10-minute mini-lesson, after which your students work on their own pieces. During writing time the classroom buzzes with a low level of productive noise. You circulate to check writing progress, confer with individual students or groups, provide guidance, and answer questions. Your students may be involved with various activities, including prewriting, drafting, reading, revising, editing, or conferring with you, a partner, or a peer group. The entire classroom is utilized, with activities taking place at the students' desks, at tables, or at your desk.

Writing is a powerful tool for learning. It enables us to analyze and synthesize our thoughts, and thereby discover new ideas. When we write we become conscious of ourselves. We define ourselves, and we come to understand our lives. Through the writing workshop, you will help your students master the skills that will enable them to express themselves with clarity and competence.

THE WRITING PROCESS

Traditional writing instruction focuses on teaching students the features of different types of writing through examples. The theory assumes that once students understand the different models—for example, narratives, editorials, essays, and various kinds of fiction—they will be able to write them.

The writing process, however, concentrates on the way real writers work. Writing is a process composed of at least five stages: prewriting, drafting, revising, editing, and publishing. Although the stages are distinct, the process is recursive. Authors will often move back and forth through the various stages as they work.

Prewriting is the starting point. It is the period during which an author discovers his or her topic, decides on his or her audience and purpose, generates ideas, and considers a form for his or her writing.

Drafting begins when the author starts writing. During this stage the author switches between writing and reading. She may rewrite some of her work or reformulate her original ideas and return to the prewriting stage.

Revising follows drafting and includes adding, deleting, rewriting, and polishing. Authors may move back through drafting and prewriting several times as they rethink their work and revise.

The *editing* stage is the final preparation for publishing. This is the time any remaining corrections of mechanics are made and the piece is put into its finished form. Even here, though, writers may decide that more revision is necessary and shift back to some of the previous stages.

Publishing refers to the sharing of writing with someone. For students this most often is teachers, peers, parents, or the public. It may also include submitting material to magazines, newspapers, or newsletters.

While I have taught writing since 1975, using a variety of programs and methods, the best writing of my students has come out of my writing workshop. In a writing workshop students spend the greatest amount of their time developing ideas, organizing information, and *writing*. The writing workshop provides the environment for students to learn the skills of written language, focus their attention on writing, and express their ideas and feelings through their finished pieces.

YOUR NEW ROLE

You will become nurturer, facilitator, and promoter in your writing workshop. No longer will you be a mere giver of information. Aside from mini-lessons, your time will be spent working with individuals and small groups. And since modeling can be a powerful motivator and teacher, on occasion you may write along with your students.

You will be performing many tasks in your writing workshop. During the class, you might help one student narrow his topic, suggest ways in which another can improve her opening, listen to yet another as she explains how she intends to develop her narrative about moving into a new home. From there you might meet with a group that is sharing drafts, seeking peer reactions. You will guide, encourage, and applaud students in their writing efforts and help them discover new insights, make connections between ideas, analyze information, and communicate their thoughts and feelings. You will give them personal feedback that reinforces their learning. The accompanying list, "The Teacher's Role in the Writing Workshop," suggests some of the many possible activities.

Teachers who are starting writing workshops often express three major concerns. The first is the worry that as they circulate around the room helping individuals and small-group members, the other students will stop working and become disruptive. The second worry is that the writing workshop may run fine with small classes but not with large ones. The third is ensuring that all students will have an opportunity to learn the skills necessary for effective writing.

A well-run workshop overcomes all these fears because the students become involved with their writing. Given the chance and encouragement to express themselves—to share of themselves—students become more willing to write. When students are involved with the class, disruption is reduced.

You ensure the dissemination of information and skills through your mini-lessons. The material imparted at the beginning of each class eventually builds a foundation of knowledge that can be referred to during individual and group conferences. Thus the material introduced is reinforced throughout the year.

Of course, as in any class, rules must be made and expectations set and expressed. These basics are up to each teacher, and you should set the rules for your classroom in a way you feel comfortable. At the least you should insist that talking is to be done in quiet voices, that there is to be no running or shoving, and that only writing-related activities may be done in the writing workshop. (For more information on discipline, see "When Discipline Is Necessary" in Section 2.)

A MODEL OF THE TYPICAL WRITING WORKSHOP

Every writing workshop reflects the personality and attitudes of its teacher. You will no doubt develop your workshop in a way that best meets the needs of your particular students and teaching environment. There are, in fact, many variations of the writing workshop; they differ slightly in structure but not content. The model presented here is one of the more common ones.

The writing workshop starts with a 5- to 10-minute mini-lesson. Each mini-lesson focuses on one skill or concept. The students may use the information of the mini-lesson right away or maybe not for several days or even weeks.

After the mini-lesson, students work on their writing for approximately 20 to 25 minutes. They may be writing in journals, searching through idea folders, or writing a story or article. It is unlikely that all students will be doing the same thing. During this time, the teacher circulates around the room and works with individual students

The Teacher's Role
in the Writing Workshop

At the beginning of the writing workshop the teacher may present a mini-lesson and then spend the rest of the period engaged in any or all of the following:

- Helping students find topics.
- Helping students focus topics.
- Answering student questions about writing.
- Guiding students in research efforts.
- Listening to a student read a paragraph.
- Offering suggestions for revision.
- Working with a group brainstorming ideas.
- Showing a student how to reduce clutter in his writing.
- Helping a student organize her ideas.
- Writing along with students.
- Offering encouragement.
- Applauding a student's efforts.
- Conferring with students over finished pieces.
- Helping a student sort through his thoughts.
- Explaining the use of a thesaurus.
- Directing traffic flow around the room.
- Reminding students of classroom rules.
- Keeping students on task.
- Helping a student cut and paste during revision.
- Assisting students in creating a class magazine.
- Helping students who are working with word processors.

and small groups. Along with providing help and encouragement, she will also remind students of the rules of the classroom and keep them on task.

The last 10 to 15 minutes of the class are reserved for sharing. This may be done via the author's chair or through peer groups. For the author's chair, students take center stage and read their work to the class. Students may first describe what they have been working on and then read from their work in progress. The rest of the class listens and may ask questions or offer suggestions. For peer groups, students read their work to members of small groups. Group members may comment on the student's work, and the student may ask for their advice or reactions. (For more information about peer groups, see "Peer Conferences" in Section 5.)

Here is a breakdown for a 45-minute period:

Mini-lesson—5 to 10 minutes
Writing Time—20 to 25 minutes
Sharing—10 to 15 minutes

There is much variation. Some teachers offer mini-lessons every other day; some teachers prefer to include a 10-minute silent writing time after the mini-lesson and reduce the writing and sharing time; some schedule sharing for only two or three days per week. You should organize your workshop in a way that is most effective for you and your students.

I like to have all students share after each class because sharing provides closure and keeps the students moving forward. Some students, if they find that there is no sharing that day, will ease off in their work. I encourage students to share even if they merely tell their peer group how they searched for a topic. Working together like this promotes an atmosphere of friendship and support as well as helps to spread understanding of the writing process. In time you are likely to see a company of writers emerge in your classroom.

PROMOTING YOUR WRITING WORKSHOP

Unless your district has made a commitment to implement writing workshops in place of traditional English classes, you will probably need to promote and explain what you are doing to administrators, colleagues, and parents. You may find some resistance at first, because the writing workshop is quite different from classes in which the teacher stands before the students, offers information through lectures, and then assigns homework that reinforces the skills taught during the lesson. The writing workshop instead fosters a learning environment in which self-discovery and cooperation become paramount.

The best way to explain the writing workshop to administrators, supervisors, and colleagues is to invite them into your class; describe what is going on; and let them see how the workshop functions. Invite them back for additional visits so that they can gain an understanding of the many activities that are a part of your workshop. Sharing samples of your students' writing, either individual papers or class magazines, is a way to show the results of your workshop.

You should inform parents about your writing workshop early in the school year. At back-to-school night I tell the parents of my students that I will be teaching a writing workshop instead of the traditional English class. I explain what the writing workshop is and mention that it is being used successfully throughout the country. I emphasize that their children will continue to learn the skills for effective language, including grammar, punctuation, and spelling. The single greatest concern parents have is that their children may learn to write but will not learn grammar. To many parents, writing and grammar are separate disciplines. I explain that they are inseparable. One will never write effectively without understanding grammar, but knowing grammar without being able to apply it to written language is a useless skill. Sending home copies of student magazines, making sure that the writing of your students appears in school and PTA newsletters, and liberally exhibiting your students' work on hallway bulletin boards can quicken the acceptance of your workshop.

In many cases your students will become the advocates of your writing workshop. Their enthusiasm for the workshop will be clear, and they will speak well of it to others. That, coupled with samples of their writing, will be your strongest promotion.

When students write about topics that interest them in an environment that supports the risk taking that is vital to conceiving and developing fresh ideas, their minds and imaginations become involved with their material. When they know that their work will be shared, that others will read what they have written, and that their writing matters, they strive for precision and clarity. Of all the advantages the writing workshop offers, perhaps these are most important.

2

Managing the Writing Workshop

Successful writing workshops, in large part, are the result of effective management. Although the structure of the writing workshop is different from that of the traditional English class, you are still responsible for sustaining a learning atmosphere, monitoring and evaluating student progress, maintaining discipline, teaching new skills, imparting information, and communicating with administrators, colleagues, and parents. You have the obligations of a traditional classroom teacher, with the added task of running a program in which students are working on a variety of topics.

In the beginning of the school year, students will have countless questions, especially if they have never participated in the writing workshop before. With the press of questions for the teacher and the new type of class for the students, it is easy for everyone to feel overwhelmed.

On the first day, you should explain the writing process and the writing workshop. Describe your expectations and how the workshop will be run. You might distribute copies of the accompanying "Student Responsibilities in the Writing Workshop" and discuss it with your students. Show them where writing materials and reference books are. If you have time, you might get students started right away by brainstorming topics with the class and encouraging students to choose their own for writing. Getting everyone involved that first day is a fine start. It shows that writing is the purpose of the class.

You will find that much of what you tell your students on this first day will need to be repeated. However, as students become more familiar with the classroom routines, they will have fewer questions on procedures, and you will have more time to work with them on their writing.

Student Responsibilities in the Writing Workshop

This year you will be taking part in a writing workshop. As in any class, you will assume various responsibilities. To ensure a successful experience in the writing workshop you should:

- Maintain a writing folder in which you will keep your writing.
- Bring your writing folder to class each day.
- Come to class each day ready to write.
- Find and develop topics for your writing.
- Be willing to try new kinds of writing.
- Do your best to learn the rules of written English.
- Accept the responsibility of completing pieces.
- Be willing to try new techniques, methods, and strategies to improve your writing.
- Be willing to work with your peers in the learning of writing skills and strategies.
- Behave properly. This means following directions and not disturbing others.
- Take pride in your work and produce the best work you can.
- Grow as a writer.

*STRUCTURING YOUR WORKSHOP*_____

Writing workshops that buzz with the activity of students working on a variety of tasks may, to the uninitiated, appear to be disorganized and chaotic. In fact, most of these classrooms are built on a firm underlying structure. A reasonable and efficient system of management is essential for the writing workshop to run smoothly.

Perhaps most important to management is a set schedule. While the ideal is to set up your writing workshop for a full period, five days per week, many teachers do not have that amount of time. You can run a fine workshop meeting three or four times a week, but at fewer than three you will have trouble maintaining continuity and keeping your students interested. Some teachers incorporate the writing workshop with their English classes. Assuming they meet five days per week, they may use three classes for the workshop and spend the other two on literature or spelling and other language skills. Here too, however, at fewer than three meetings per week, it will be difficult to sustain the thought and emotion necessary for a good writing workshop.

When students know that they have writing workshop each day, or every Monday, Tuesday, and Thursday, for example, they will come to the workshop ready to write. When students meet regularly for writing workshop, their minds become engaged with the writing process.

In schools where it is impossible to meet regularly for the writing workshop throughout the year, the workshop may be scheduled for fixed meetings during part of the year. The writing workshop may rotate with courses like computer literacy, music, art, home economics, or industrial arts for sessions that span several weeks. Regular meetings during an 8- to 10-week period are preferable to irregular or limited meetings throughout the year.

*CREATING AND MAINTAINING A WRITING ENVIRONMENT*_____

The environment you set up for your students tells much about your attitude toward writing. A classroom that is bright and cheerful, where fresh ideas, openness, and sharing are energetically promoted, where encouragement and support are offered, elevates the importance of writing in the eyes of students.

You should do as much as possible to create and maintain a classroom that is conducive to writing. If you store students' writing folders in a box, for example, cover the box with colorful paper or fabric and file the folders alphabetically for easy retrieval. Encourage students to keep their folders neat and avoid merely cramming work into them. You might assign a different student each week to monitor the folder box and make sure that the folders are put back the right way. Instruct students to put their names, dates, and sections on their papers; staple the pages; and label them "Draft" or "Final Copy." When your actions communicate to students that you expect quality work, you are more likely to get it.

Encourage your students to treat resource and writing materials with the same respect. Set up a writer's library at one corner of the classroom and stock it with dictionaries, thesauruses, rhyming dictionaries, style books, and other references. Making references available supports students in their efforts to find their own answers to questions. Also, make available such items as paper, pencils, pens, markers, glue, and scissors. Allow students to use these materials as necessary, but instruct them to put things back when done. As with their folders, you might assign a different student each week to make sure that the materials are returned at the end of each period. To ensure that everyone understands how to handle the materials, you may discuss the rules during one of your class meetings.

Students also need to be instructed how to move through the class. Ideally, the writing workshop has desks as well as tables for both individual and group work. If your classroom is like mine, the ideal is seldom the reality. It is likely that students will need to move their chairs to tables and slide desks together when working in groups. To reduce the disruption, encourage your students to move chairs and materials quietly and carefully. If you have a large class, you might have them move into their groups by section. Letting the left side of the room go first, then the right, eliminates a mass of jumbled bodies moving in different directions at once. When students must consult a dictionary, get paper, or work with scissors and paste, remind them not to stop along the way and visit with their friends. Writing is the priority in the writing workshop. You may find that you will need to remind students of these basics often, but it is necessary. Much time can be lost and many disruptions can occur as students move around the room.

There *will* be some noise in the writing workshop. Students will need to get more paper, share a draft with an editing partner, confer with you about the lead of a story, or check references. You must decide how much of the activity is purposeful and how much is mere clatter. There will be times when you will have to refocus your students. Often, a reminder, "Let's remember to use our soft voices," is enough. Sometimes you may have to speak with students individually. You should also have students keep their desks clear of everything except writing materials. Since there will be movement throughout the class, nonessential books on desks invariably get knocked down, causing noise and confusion.

There is a lot of group work during most writing workshops. Students regularly confer with partners and peers about their writing. This can be a management challenge. At the beginning of the year, I share my rules for working in groups during a mini-lesson. The following rules may be applied to all group situations. For additional information on group work see "Peer Group Guidelines" in Section 5.

Explain to your students that the purpose of meeting in groups is to share ideas. Adhering to common-sense procedures when working together helps ensure that important ideas are discussed. Distribute copies of the accompanying "Rules for Working in Groups" and discuss the rules with your students.

Modeling a group working together in front of the class is a good way to show students how a group should function. You may take part in the group or act as a director, guiding students in their roles. During group activities, especially in the beginning of the year, you will likely have to circulate from group to group offering guidance.

To help your groups work effectively, you can assign roles. One student is the leader, another the coleader, a third the recorder, a fourth a noise-level monitor, and a fifth the timekeeper. The roles change with each group activity. Assigning roles gives each student a specific share in the group and responsibility for its effectiveness.

You may find that you will have to remind students of the rules for effective group work often in the early part of the year. But once they realize that you expect and demand this behavior, your group will function more smoothly.

Organize your classroom so that students find it easy to write and confer within the patterns of a predictable routine. Within an environment that promotes consistency, creativity and industry will flourish.

The Writing Environment

Following are some elements of a classroom that is designed for writing:

- The classroom is bright and cheerful.
- Fresh ideas, openness, and sharing are promoted.
- The classroom is designed to facilitate the writing effort. Folders are kept in a separate box; reference books and materials for writing are available.
- Students are encouraged to do their best work.
- Papers are headed and labeled.
- Students move through the classroom showing consideration for others.
- Noise is purposeful.
- Students are involved with a variety of tasks—writing, revising, sharing a draft with a friend, conferring with a teacher, brainstorming for ideas.
- Writing enjoys priority.
- Writing is treated as a process including these stages: prewriting, drafting, revising, editing, and publishing.

Rules for Working in Groups

To help make sure that your group works productively, follow these points:

- Every student should participate in the sharing of ideas.
- Speakers should think about the points they wish to make before speaking.
- After stating their points, speakers should give the floor to someone else.
- Group members should listen politely to others.
- The discussion should be about writing.
- Questions should be appropriate and on the topic.
- Listeners should not interrupt speakers. If they have questions, they should ask after the speaker is done.
- If a listener disagrees with a speaker, he or she should explain why in a calm, clear manner.
- Comments should always be positive and constructive.

*PLANNING YOUR WORKSHOP LESSONS*_____

Mini-lessons are the most efficient way of imparting information to the whole class in the writing workshop. The typical mini-lesson runs between 5 and 10 minutes and focuses on one topic or skill. That amount of time is usually sufficient to cover the material. Longer lessons take too much time away from writing.

A question that often arises is how to write plans for the writing workshop in a plan book. An example is shown in the accompanying box.

Monday

Mini-lesson:	Writing personal narratives.
Procedure:	Students work individually or in groups.
Closing:	Peer group engages in sharing.

Tuesday

Mini-lesson:	Effective leads.
Procedure:	Students work individually or in groups.
Closing:	Two or three students share their work from the author's chair.

Wednesday

Mini-lesson:	Sentence constructions.
Procedure:	Students work individually or in groups.
Closing:	Peer group engages in sharing.

Thursday

Mini-lesson:	Sentence fragments.
Procedure:	Students work individually or in groups.
Closing:	Two or three students share their work from the author's chair.

Friday

Mini-lesson:	Using descriptive words.
Procedure:	Students work individually or in groups.
Closing:	Peer group engages in sharing.

A mini-lesson is not the kind of lesson in which a skill or concept is taught and then every student does an assignment. Rather, they should be used to introduce new material, share techniques for improving writing, or teach the skills students need to use grammar and punctuation correctly. The information you offer through mini-lessons should always be simple and digestible. It will be reinforced during individual and group conferences.

You should select your mini-lessons based on the needs of your students. The mini-lessons throughout this kit, especially in Part II, cover many of the skills necessary for written English. However, only you will know which skills your students need, and you may want to create many of your own mini-lessons by using the mini-lessons of this kit as a guide.

*MANAGING TIME IN THE WRITING WORKSHOP*_____

The writing workshop can present you with a heavy work load. This is especially true for teachers who team teach or who are departmentalized. By managing the class and your time effectively, you will be able to handle the work.

When you set up your classroom, think in terms of efficiency. If you have more than one writing workshop, and your students are to leave their writing folders in the classroom, have a separate box for each class. Differently colored boxes make it easy for students to go directly to their folders. Have the folders arranged alphabetically and instruct your students to pick them up as they enter the room. If you are self-contained, or if you team teach and have students for a longer period, you may have a student pass out the folders instead of having each student take his or her own. Providing separate baskets for drafts and final copies (you can even do this by class) reduces work by keeping papers in distinct piles. You can reduce work further by making writing materials accessible to students. Encouraging students to use materials as necessary cuts down on countless questions such as, "May I have the 'White out'?" "Where are the scissors?" and "May I borrow a pen?" which will intrude on the time you could be helping students with their writing.

Along with arranging your classroom for efficiency, establish procedures that foster independence and cooperation. Set up peer groups and conference partners so that students can share their writing and help each other. (See "Peer Conferences" in Section 5.) Much learning occurs through sharing. To avoid long lines at your desk, move around the classroom and work with students at their desks or tables.

Grading papers can be the biggest part of your work load. Avoid grading every paper, which is unrealistic because a given student's pieces vary in quality just as the works of professional writers do. Moreover, when students feel that they won't be immediately graded on a paper, they are more likely to take risks with their writing and experiment with new forms.

Never take everyone's papers home at one time. Distribute the grading activity over several nights or a few nights per week. When you take home too much, you'll only overwhelm yourself and probably not read any of them. The papers will only pile up even higher.

Students can help you in your efforts to make the workshop efficient. Appoint students to check materials and make sure that items are put back. You might label the number of items that belong in a box to make it easier to keep track of inventory. For example, if you have 12 scissors, mark 12 on the box so that the monitor knows how many scissors should be returned and will not have to ask you how many items should be there. At the end of the period if all items are not returned, remind the class that some things are missing and ask them to find it. Knowing that materials will be closely monitored discourages their disappearance. (Of course, even if you do not designate student monitors, you should still check your inventory of materials at the end of each period to make sure that you do not lose supplies.) If you prefer to hand out the writing folders at the beginning of the period, let students do it. This will free you to settle the class and start the workshop a little sooner. If you are using skills analysis sheets (see "Evaluation" in this section) for recordkeeping, allow students to contribute as much information as possible. They can at least put their names, sections, and topics on the sheets. Having plenty of sheets copied in advance and available allows students to fill out the sheets as needed.

A writing workshop that has a clear, simple structure with organized routines will function more smoothly than one in which organization is lacking. A smooth-running workshop will allow you to spend more time with students and work on their writing skills.

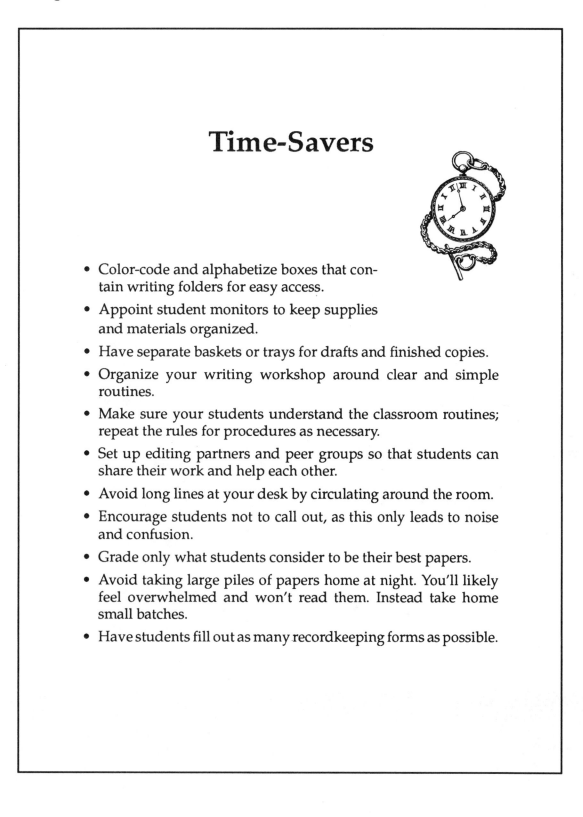

Time-Savers

- Color-code and alphabetize boxes that contain writing folders for easy access.
- Appoint student monitors to keep supplies and materials organized.
- Have separate baskets or trays for drafts and finished copies.
- Organize your writing workshop around clear and simple routines.
- Make sure your students understand the classroom routines; repeat the rules for procedures as necessary.
- Set up editing partners and peer groups so that students can share their work and help each other.
- Avoid long lines at your desk by circulating around the room.
- Encourage students not to call out, as this only leads to noise and confusion.
- Grade only what students consider to be their best papers.
- Avoid taking large piles of papers home at night. You'll likely feel overwhelmed and won't read them. Instead take home small batches.
- Have students fill out as many recordkeeping forms as possible.

KEEPING STUDENTS MOTIVATED

I've never met a teacher of writing who has not heard students complain about writing.

"It's boring . . ."

"Do we have to write?"

"I can't think of anything to write about."

"Why do we have to do this?"

While you will be hearing these kinds of complaints much less in the writing workshop than you would in a traditional writing class, you will still hear them from some students. Usually, these students have a reason for not wanting to write. The complaint may be a disguise for the real reason. Perhaps they believe that they have nothing to write about, they may feel that their classmates won't accept what they write, or their reluctance may have roots in a lack of self-worth, hardships at home, learning disabilities, or problems at school.

When trying to motivate students to write, the carrot is better than the stick. Provide plenty of encouragement, praise, and support. Try to boost the self-image of these students. It is especially important to help them find topics and build ideas. Everyone has hundreds of stories to tell. These students need to be shown that others are interested in what they have to say.

Reluctant writers also benefit from the support of their peers. Whenever possible, put them in groups where they will receive support. Build a classroom environment where they feel safe enough to share their ideas. For these students a classroom that has a firm structure and steady routines is vital. Such a classroom offers a safe haven in which they are more likely to write and experiment with ideas.

For every student who does not want to write, there will be several who will embrace your workshop with vigor and passion. However, even your most motivated students will vary in the quality of the work they produce. All authors experience highs and lows. You will likely see growth come in spurts, with some backsliding in between. This is normal, even for your top students.

You can also expect to see a wide diversity in the abilities and skills of your students. Young authors develop at different rates. They are individuals and their skills grow individually. You can guide learning, but you can't rush it.

WHEN DISCIPLINE IS NECESSARY

No matter how smoothly your writing workshop runs, there will be times that you will need to discipline students. Never ignore discipline in the hopes that the workshop setting will miraculously solve problems. Although your role changes with the writing workshop, you are still the teacher, and you must not hesitate to correct students for inappropriate behavior.

They may not understand why they misbehave, but most students have a reason for disrupting class. They may be seeking attention or power, lacking self-esteem, or acting out anger. You should learn to identify these students and address any disruption immediately. Stay calm in handling discipline because anger on your part only worsens matters. Not only will you be able to manage disruptions more effectively by remaining calm, but you will make a stronger impression on the rest of the class. For severe behavior problems, you should not hesitate to utilize the typical disciplinary procedures of your school, which may include detention, intervention by the principal, and parent conferences.

When forced to discipline, try to separate it from writing. Isolate the behavior that needs correction and address that. Once the incident has been addressed, refocus the student on his or her work. This reinforces the importance of writing.

Following are several common discipline problems you are likely to face in the writing workshop and suggestions how to solve them. For the student who:

- **Does not complete pieces.**

   Speak to him individually about the importance of starting and finishing pieces. Monitor his daily work closely. If necessary, set reasonable deadlines that the first draft must be done by, for example, Tuesday, with the final finished by Thursday. If the student fails to make the deadline, he must stay after school or give up a free period. Treat him just as you would any other student who does not finish assignments.

- **Is easily distracted.**

   Speak to this student about keeping her attention on task. Place this student's desk at a front corner of the classroom and surround her with quiet students, preferably those who will do little to distract her. For group work, place this student with those who are likely to remain on task. Providing her with good models will foster appropriate behavior.

- **Writes on inappropriate topics or with inappropriate language.**

   Speak to this student privately and explain your standards of appropriateness. You might ask why he is writing the way he is. If you can uncover the reason, you will be better able to address the issue and change the behavior. Often students will write on inappropriate topics or use offensive language out of anger or frustration or merely as a test to see how much you will tolerate. If the student continues to write like that after you have spoken to him, you should consider contacting his parent or guardian. Confronting this problem quickly, calmly, and firmly usually leads to a solution. (*Note:* Sometimes writing or talking inappropriately about sexuality is a sign of sexual abuse. If you suspect abuse, you should report it to your supervisor.)

- **Criticizes or mocks others orally or in writing.**

   If the student does this openly in front of the class, you should address it before the class. Immediately intercede and explain that negative criticism or mockery is not acceptable. No one has the right to hurt another's feelings. Ask the student to imagine herself in the place of those she has mocked. What would her feelings be? Her quick answer may be, "I wouldn't care," but counter that by telling her that you know she would. You might also mention that the purpose of the writing workshop is to help people learn the skills for effective language use. Everyone's efforts in the class should be directed to that purpose.

   If the student criticizes or mocks others in her writing, speak to her privately. Stress the importance of providing support and encouragement to others rather than denigrating the student or her work.

- **Writes about students or teachers.**

    In the beginning of the year I tell my students that one of the rules of the writing workshop is that students do not use other students or teachers in their writing without the other person's permission. Sometimes students write narratives in which friends were involved; however, the rule makes it clear that writing about others without first asking is not acceptable. When a student ignores the rule, you can speak to him individually, reminding him that no one has the right to make someone uncomfortable by using him in a story he doesn't want to be in.

- **Refuses to share her writing.**

    Sometimes a student may refuse to share her work because she feels that it isn't good enough or it may be private. If it is private, don't insist that she share. However, if she feels that the work is not good enough, you might have her read her writing to you first. Work with the student to improve the piece; then provide plenty of support for her to share. Placing this student in a peer group composed of students with similar abilities will make her feel less threatened than being in a group of the class's best writers. If the student is still reluctant to share, suggest that she read only an opening or merely talk about her piece. If she still hesitates, ask her if you can share her work with the class for her. Once her work is shared, the second presentation will be easier to arrange.

- **Dominates sharing during peer groups.**

    To rein in a student who tries to dominate sharing, you might place him with an equally forceful dominating student in a group. Avoid putting the dominating student with a group that will accommodate him. If necessary, you should sit in on the group, model the appropriate behavior, and act as the monitor. You may have to do this a few times so that students understand the procedures and goals of a peer group. (See "Peer Groups" in Section 5.)

- **Confers much but accomplishes little.**

    Separate this student from group work unless essential. When organizing groups, put this student with others who are likely to stay on task. You might also impose deadlines to keep this student working.

- **Demands constant attention.**

    When a student demands your attention constantly, you must remind him, calmly, but strongly, that you are working with someone else and that you will help him as soon as possible. Direct him back to his task by suggesting that he work with a peer or consult reference materials while he is waiting for you. Permitting this student to stand beside you as you help another will only encourage his demands.

- **Lacks patience (for example, cannot wait for her turn to use the computer).**

    When a student is impatient, speak to her individually and explain that everyone must have a turn. If necessary, address the class on the issue via a mini-lesson on procedure. It is important that you maintain strict rules on patience and sharing. If you ignore the rules for one, you will be expected to ignore the rules for all. If impatience continues to be a problem, consult a counselor, as the student may be having emotional problems.

- **Has trouble sharing materials.**

    Speak to this student about the need for sharing. If several students have this same problem, you may want to talk about it to the entire class by way of a procedural mini-lesson.

- **Plagiarizes.**

    Plagiarism is a serious issue. Speak to the student individually and explain that plagiarism is the taking of another's writing and using it as one's own. Mention that by plagiarizing, the student is not being fair to herself. She is not allowing herself the opportunity to learn to express herself with her own words. Mini-lesson 41 of Part II concerns plagiarism.

- **Keeps writing the same type of pieces and refuses to move on to other kinds of writing.**

    This student needs support and encouragement. Often the reason for not moving on is safety. Moving on may mean taking risks, which some students are reluctant to do. To help overcome this obstacle, try brainstorming ideas for different types of writing. A good time to do this is after explaining new types of writing during mini-lessons. (See "Types of Writing," Mini-lessons 1 to 16, in Part II.) You can follow the mini-lesson with brainstorming for topics. This may provide the boost the student needs to launch into new writing forms.

- **Has indecipherable handwriting.**

    If the student has a motor coordination problem, and if you have a word processor in your classroom, let the student write stories on the word processor. If that is not possible, the student may be able to dictate a story that you or a volunteer can write down. Our school utilizes community volunteers who help in such situations.

    Of course, sometimes the handwriting of students is a result of carelessness or not caring. In such cases, speak to the student about being neater. Suggest that he slow down and form his letters more carefully. Explain that illegible handwriting detracts from his work. Ask him why someone would want to spend the time trying to read writing that is illegible.

    Some students need incentives to write neatly. I recall one boy whose handwriting was so sloppy that he often had trouble reading his own words. When given the chance to put his work in a class magazine—provided his writing was legible—his handwriting improved dramatically.

- **Is being helped by a parent or older sibling.**

    Encouraging your students to do most of their writing in school helps to eliminate this problem. For students who insist on doing much of their writing at home, and who you believe are not turning in their own work, confront them and ask. While few students will admit that someone else did their work, many will concede that they had help. At this admission, you should explain that only by doing their own work can they expect to learn good writing skills.

    In some cases, you may have to contact the student's parent. Be tactful. It won't do to call and bluntly accuse the parent of doing her child's work. Rather, mention that you notice a difference in the quality of her child's work done in school compared to the quality of the work finished at home. You can then bring up the subject of help. Explain that while help is important, and you appreciate the parent's concern for the child's achievement, emphasize that it is also important that the student does her own work. Not only will she learn more writing skills, but she will feel ownership of the work and will likely take more pride in it.

- **Is disruptive.**

   Address the disruptive behavior. Speak to the student and explain why the behavior will not be tolerated. You might also mention the consequences if it happens again. If the behavior continues, utilize the disciplinary procedures of your school, which might include time after school, detention, or calling parents. I speak to such students in private and will ask them for suggestions how we can work together to improve their behavior. Some students will tell you why they are misbehaving, which will help you to modify their classroom interaction and thereby improve their behavior. Frequently, just talking and drawing the student out makes a difference, because the student sees that you care about him.

- **Is not working because of an undiagnosed learning problem.**

   You should contact your child study team or your administrator in charge of learning disabilities and recommend that the student be tested to discover if any learning problems exist. Delay will only cause frustration to the student who is having trouble working successfully in your writing workshop because of a learning problem.

Individual students should never be permitted to disrupt the writing workshop. Misbehavior affects not only the individual but those around him. In most cases, following common sense and being consistent in discipline will serve you well.

EVALUATION

Evaluating the writing of students is always difficult because it is a subjective process. No matter how hard a teacher may try to read a paper objectively, he invariably evaluates with his biases and preconceptions. Just as readers may disagree over the merits of the same book, teachers often disagree over the strengths and weaknesses of a student's writing.

Evaluating according to specific criteria promotes objectivity. When you determine grades by looking for consistent elements in papers, you are likely to be more objective in evaluation. When I grade, I concentrate on five major areas: focus, content, organization, style, and mechanics. A well-written paper will be strong in all areas.

Some teachers choose, or are required, to give grades in numerical values. While it is certainly more difficult to do that for writing than for other subjects, referring to the following percentage breakdown of a piece's major elements can be helpful.

Focus: The topic is clearly defined, and all ideas relate to the topic. (*20 percent*)
Content: The student uses fresh, insightful, or original ideas. The topic is developed and supported with details. (*25 percent*)
Organization: The piece progresses logically from beginning to end. For nonfiction, an interesting introduction, body, and satisfying ending can be easily identified. For fiction, an interesting opening, development, and climax are apparent. (*25 percent*)

Style: The writing is appropriate for the topic and audience. There is a distinct voice and effective imagery. (*15 percent*)
Mechanics: The writer uses correct punctuation, grammar, and spelling. (*15 percent*)

I like to base the grades of my students on five papers each per marking period and allow them to select the ones they want me to mark. My only requirement is that each piece is a different type of writing. For example, I will not accept five personal narratives for grading from a student.

Requiring five pieces for grading takes into account that students, like adults, vary in the quality of their work. Some topics will fire their imagination while others—which may have seemed like good ideas—fail to sustain the interest necessary to complete successfully. Counting every paper in the final grade inhibits some students from taking risks with their writing. Rather than trying something new, which might result in a low grade, these students will keep writing the same things to get their "A." I grade only final copies, but encourage students to finish all the pieces they begin. Before they do their final drafts, I confer with students individually, offering any last suggestions for revision. When grading a final, I read through it to get a feel for its overall scope; then I reread it for content and mechanics. I base the grade on the overall paper. Since I have been working with the students throughout the development of their pieces, I am familiar with their work and grading is fairly easy.

Evaluation should not be just a form of criticism, but rather should aim to boost students in their growth as writers. It should always be based on what has been taught, and it must be consistent. I explain to my students how their grades will be determined on the first or second day of school, and I explain that to their parents on back-to-school night. Students deserve to know ahead of time how their grades will be determined.

While my school has interim reports, I also send parents notes when their children fall behind in their work. I require that the notes be signed and returned so that I have proof that the parent actually saw the note. Some parents hear from me by the end of the first week of school, and every year a few acquire a quasi pen-pal status. When parents are kept informed of what their children are doing, they are more likely to support your efforts. While not all parents will be helpful, by keeping them informed you will at least reduce the chance that they will be "surprised" by their child's grade.

MONITORING THE PROGRESS OF YOUR STUDENTS

Since your students will be working at their own rates, you must monitor their progress closely to ensure that they complete pieces in a timely manner. You must also be aware of the skills they have acquired and the ones that remain to be learned.

If you wish to record the daily progress of your students, there are several methods you can utilize. One option is to maintain a daily log. Set up on a weekly basis, and using a code that appears on the bottom of the page, you can record each student's topic and what he or she has accomplished. Reviewing your daily log is one way to follow the progress of your students. Observation as you circulate around the room during writing is another. Unless a piece is complicated or goes through several hard revisions, or the student has been absent, I expect a finished piece about every five class periods. I tell my students that this is a time frame to aim for and that it will result in their completing enough pieces for grading. For students who have trouble finishing pieces, I will require that they complete at least one piece every two weeks.

The daily log is also useful for encouraging students to come to class with a plan for writing. If they know that you recorded what they did yesterday, they know you will be expecting them to move ahead today. Keeping the log handy as you move around the room makes recordkeeping easy. Following is a sample portion of a log. (A reproducible blank log sheet is also provided.)

Daily Log

	Student	Topic	\multicolumn{5}{c}{Dates}
			10/14	10/15	10/16	10/17	10/18
1.	A. Buetell	Fishing Trip	D^1	TC/R	D^2	EP	F
2.	J. Callahan	Limericks	P	P	D	PC	TC/R
3.	R. Cortland	The Grind/Parents	F	P	D	TC/R	F
4.	S. Dove	The Lost Puppy	TC/P	D	PC	R	E/F

Codes:

P	–	Prewriting		EP	–	Editing (Partners)
D	–	Draft		R	–	Revision
PC	–	Peer Conference		F	–	Final Copy
TC	–	Teacher Conference		NC	–	Work Not Completed
E	–	Editing (Self)				

Another method of charting the progress of your students is use of the accompanying "Skills Analysis Sheet." These charts can be used to record the skills on specific pieces, or they can be used as general records after every two or three pieces. Typical sheets are divided into categories for which you would log strengths and weaknesses as well as the suggestions for improvement. Skills analysis sheets enable you to follow closely the growth of students' writing.

Along with recording the skills your students acquire, it is important that they try different types of writing. Without a gentle nudge from their teachers, some students will only write poems, others only personal narratives, and still others only essays. I once had a boy who only wanted to write reviews of video games.

The accompanying "Checklist for Types of Writing" provides a way to ensure that your students try a variety of different kinds of writing. The checklist is designed for students to keep in their writing folders. When they finish one of the forms of writing, you initial the space. Allowing the students to keep the checklist in their folders enables them to see what forms they need to try and also eliminates my having to store the lists. (Keep the lists, however, for students who lose or misplace theirs.) Once a student's checklist is completed, collect and save it for your records.

To encourage students to try various forms of writing, introduce new types of writing via mini-lessons (see "Types of Writing" in Part II). Encourage students to try the most recently discussed writing form for their next piece, although you need not

Daily Log

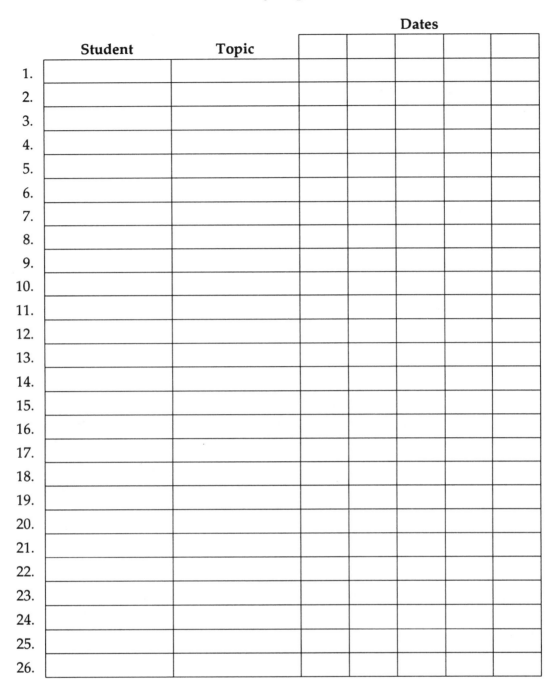

	Student	Topic	Dates				
1.							
2.							
3.							
4.							
5.							
6.							
7.							
8.							
9.							
10.							
11.							
12.							
13.							
14.							
15.							
16.							
17.							
18.							
19.							
20.							
21.							
22.							
23.							
24.							
25.							
26.							

Codes:

P	–	Prewriting	EP	–	Editing (Partners)
D	–	Draft	R	–	Revision
PC	–	Peer Conference	F	–	Final Copy
TC	–	Teacher Conference	NC	–	Work Not Completed
E	–	Editing (Self)			

Skills Analysis Sheet

Name _____ Date _____ Section_____

Title of Piece(s)_____

Components	Strengths	Weaknesses	Suggestions
Focus			
Content			
Structure			
Style			
Mechanics			

Notes:

Checklist for Types of Writing

Name _____ Date _____ Class _____

Narrative _____

Essay _____

How-to article _____

Newspaper article _____

Persuasive article _____

Friendly letter _____

Business letter _____

Book review _____

Movie review _____

Fiction story _____

Advertising _____

Nonrhyming poem _____

Rhyming poem _____

Play _____

Screenplay _____

Additional Forms:

_____ _____

_____ _____

_____ _____

_____ _____

demand it. Within the next few weeks, however, speak to anyone who still has not tried it and urge him or her to. While many students will try all the forms you introduce, others won't. You must decide how many you will teach and how many of the forms students will be required to try. Some teachers believe that advanced forms of writing, screenplays, for instance, are too difficult for students of low ability. However, I've found that when shown the form and given encouragement, even these students will try.

Evaluation helps students to see the strengths and weaknesses of their writing. It helps them to learn what good writing is.

WRITING ACROSS THE CURRICULUM

Writing should not be limited to the writing workshop. The writing skills your students learn with you should be carried over to their other classes.

If you have the opportunity to work with teachers of other subjects, coordinate your efforts. For example, when the social studies teacher assigns a report on Central America, you could cover the skills necessary for report writing in your mini-lessons. You might also permit your students to work on their reports during the workshop. With the reading teacher, you can collaborate on book reports. For their math classes, students might write review word problems for each other. You can work with the science teacher on the writing of lab reports or papers of inquiry. There are many possibilities.

If your school has a computer literacy teacher, you might work together in the production of a class magazine. Students can use word processing programs to write their stories and then illustrate the magazine using graphics software. Student magazines produced on computers can be quite impressive. (See Section 7, "Publishing.")

When students see the importance of writing in various classes, they realize the value of the writing workshop. That ultimately makes management of the workshop easier.

3

Prewriting

Prewriting includes all the activities and strategies that prepare an author to write. The prewriting stage of the writing process is the time when authors find and focus topics, generate and develop ideas, and decide on the best method to express their ideas to readers. Prewriting is an essential part of the writing process.

Prewriting can take many forms. While no writer uses all of them, students should recognize the various prewriting options so that they can select the ones they feel are most helpful. The value of prewriting is not in adherence to a specific plan, but in the concentrating of the writer's attention on the piece. Prewriting engages the writer's mind with the topic, fires up imagination and creativity, and provides the foundation for the writing that is to come.

PREWRITING STRATEGIES

In the broadest sense, anything that helps a writer get ready to write is a prewriting activity. A long thoughtful walk in the woods in which ideas for writing are examined might be a prewriting strategy for some authors. I know of a few authors who claim that they dream of the scenes they will write the next day. Some writers leave a topic alone for a time, hoping to develop it subconsciously while they attend to other projects. This is a prewriting strategy for them. Explain to your students that most authors rely on a number of prewriting activities. Following are some of the more common ones.

FREE WRITING

Free writing is a prewriting activity in which the author writes freely to discover and explore ideas. For many writers topics become apparent only after they have

Free-Writing Sample

Right now I'm having trouble. I can't think of anything to write. I don't have ideas. I never have ideas. When I look around the room I see everybody writing and I feel bad. Everybody has ideas. Not me. Maybe I'll have an idea later. Maybe I won't. Maybe. Maybe. Maybe..... This is so hard. Like the time I went to bat in the pee-wee league for the first time. I remember how scared I was. I was seven and the kid pitching was 9. He was good. And I was only okay.

started writing. The surprises in their writing become topics for them. The ideas obtained through free writing can be expanded and organized into compositions.

The goal of free writing is to find as many ideas as possible. Thus free writing is fast, with the writer getting down thoughts as they come. Time should not be spent on editing or revising during free writing. That can be done later. Fragments and even single words are acceptable. Because the focus is on ideas and not form, many students who may be reluctant to write are encouraged during free writing.

For the first few sessions, you should keep free writing to periods of about 5 minutes. As students learn the technique, you can gradually increase the writing time.

A variation of the typical free writing is "looping." In this method of free writing, students free write, then circle an idea they discover in their free writing, free write on this idea, circle a new (often narrower) idea, and continue the process until they have found a topic they wish to pursue.

The best way to demonstrate free writing is to model it for your students. You can free write on an overhead projector or read examples of your own free writing to them. If you wish, you can distribute copies of the accompanying "Free-Writing Sample." Discuss it with your students and point out how the writer went from having no ideas to uncovering an experience that would make a fine personal narrative. When students free write, you might wish to free write, too. There are few better ways of modeling.

Free writing eliminates excuses not to write. It provides a no-risk atmosphere for the most reluctant of your writers.

Activity 1: Free Writing

Explain to your students what free writing is, and tell them that they are going to participate in a free-writing session. Model free writing or distribute copies of the "Free-Writing Sample" so that students understand what they are to do. Encourage your students to think of a topic. For those who have trouble thinking of ideas, tell them to write "I can't think of anything" or a similar sentence until the ideas begin to flow. Assure them that keeping their pen or pencil point to the paper and moving will eventually generate ideas. Permit the session to run 5 minutes. After it is done, instruct your students to reread what they wrote and look for ideas that could become topics. (You might have them free write on one of these ideas to generate details they can use in writing a draft.)

CLUSTERING

Clustering, also known as mapping or webbing, is a form of word association that is an effective way to generate or elaborate on ideas. Some people liken it to individual brainstorming.

To use this prewriting method, students should select a topic in which they are interested, write it at the center of a sheet of paper, and then branch off from it, writing down words or phrases that they associate with the topic. When clustering, students should write rapidly. The purpose is to generate as many ideas as possible.

Sometimes students will uncover new topics from their initial idea and cluster. Some topics naturally lead to new topics. The accompanying "Sample Cluster" shows new major ideas being generated. Instruct your students to circle any ideas that may

A Sample Cluster

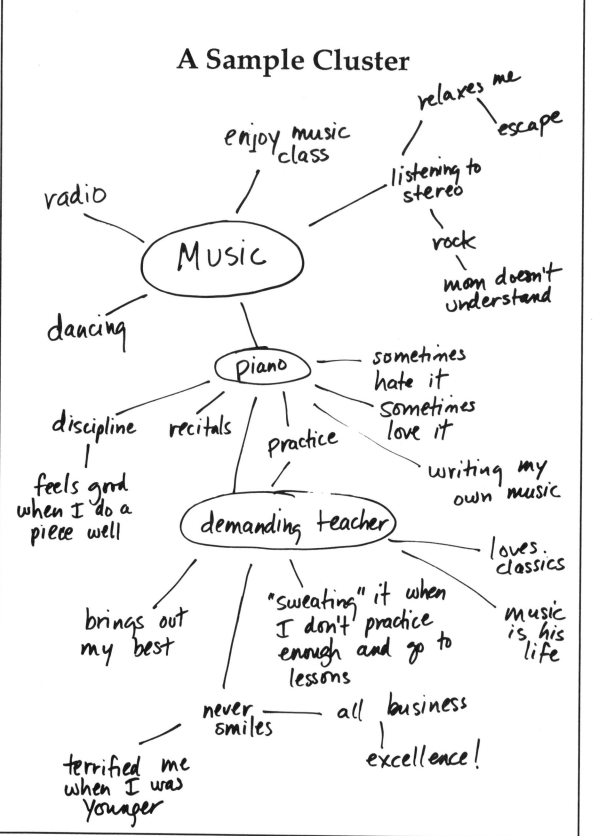

© 1993 by The Center for Applied Research in Education

be used as a topic and continue clustering. Caution your students that it is important that they narrow their topics down and focus them. Encourage them to do a second, or even third, cluster if necessary.

Activity 2: Clustering

Explain clustering to your students. Hand out copies of (or project) the "Sample Cluster" as an example. To show your students how a cluster is generated, ask them to suggest a topic and, with their help, do a cluster for it either on the board or an overhead projector. Using a topic from the students provides a good model because they know that you did not plan the cluster in advance. Also, it becomes a much more spontaneous exercise. While developing the cluster, be sure to circle any ideas that may be used as separate topics.

After you have completed the example cluster, ask your students to select a topic—you can suggest they pick an idea from their free writing—and do a cluster for it. After they have completed their clusters, ask them to write about their topics.

IDEA LISTING

Idea listing is similar to clustering. Rather than writing the topic at the center of the paper, students write it at the top of a blank sheet. They then list as many ideas as they can about the topic. It is not uncommon for idea lists to resemble clusters when they are finished.

When listing ideas, students should not worry about order or relationships, but should simply try to write as many ideas as possible. The purpose of listing is to generate ideas. Upon completion, the student reviews the ideas and selects the ones he or she wishes to develop, perhaps by clustering or free writing. While not all the ideas of the list will appear in the finished piece, many will.

Activity 3: Idea Listing

Distribute copies of the "Sample Idea List" and discuss it with your students. You should model the generation of an idea list for your students on the board or an overhead projector. Ask them to suggest a topic and offer ideas for it. This will get them involved in the process. Emphasize the similarities between idea listing and clustering. Explain that by listing as many ideas as they can about their topics, they should be able to focus their topics (discarding much of what they generated at first) and develop good compositions. After completion of the activity, instruct your students to choose a topic and generate an idea list for it. They should then write about their topics.

BRAINSTORMING

Brainstorming is a prewriting strategy in which a group quickly lists everything it can about a topic. You can utilize brainstorming with your entire class or divide your students into small groups. Effective brainstorming relies on three important rules:

Sample Idea List

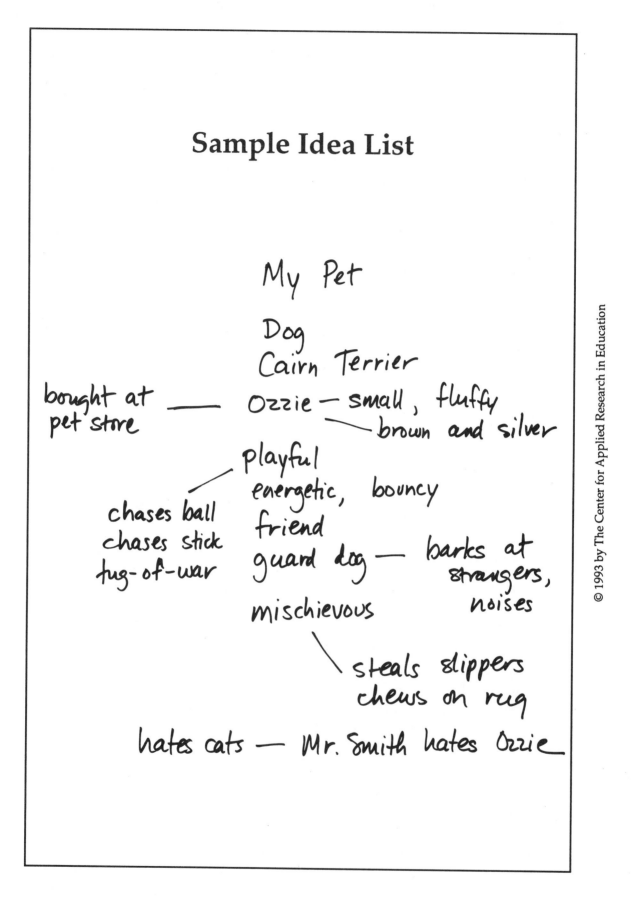

My Pet

Dog
Cairn Terrier

bought at —— Ozzie — small, fluffy
pet store   — brown and silver

chases ball   Playful
chases stick   energetic, bouncy
tug-of-war   friend
                guard dog — barks at
                              strangers,
                                  noises
                mischievous

                \ steals slippers
                  chews on rug

hates cats — Mr. Smith hates Ozzie

1. *All* ideas must be recorded.

2. Ideas should not be judged or criticized during the brainstorming session.

3. All group members should participate.

During the brainstorming, time should not be taken to analyze ideas or look for relationships. Effort should remain focused on generating ideas. After ideas are generated, instruct your students to go back over them and look for relationships and ways to expand them.

If you brainstorm with your class, you should act as the recorder. As ideas are offered, write them down either on the board or on an overhead projector. You will have to be fast because your students will be offering ideas as quickly as they can think of them. You can use brainstorming to generate topics for writing or to generate ideas about a specific topic.

When doing small-group brainstorming, I suggest you divide your students into groups of four to six. Each group should designate one student as the recorder, the person who writes down all the ideas. Other roles may also be assigned. For example, one student may be responsible for making sure that everyone contributes. Another's job may be to monitor the noise level and remind group members to quiet down when necessary. Still another's duty may be to act as moderator during the group's discussion after brainstorming, while someone else may have the task of reporting the group's findings to the class.

In setting up your groups, be sure to consider the combinations. Including a shy student with three or four vocal ones might make it impossible for the shy one to offer any ideas. One way to ensure that everyone gets a chance in the group is to have a rule that everyone must contribute at least one idea. Expect some noise, but remember that too much noise inhibits work. If you did not appoint students to be in charge of the noise level of their groups, you must watch that the noise level does not become too high and must rein your students in when it does. A preset signal—blinking the lights, ringing a small bell, or activating a beeper—can recapture the attention of your students and allow you to remind them to soften their voices.

Group brainstorming is particularly effective when students are doing similar topics or writing about different aspects of the same subject. Some groups require only a topic to begin an enthusiastic brainstorming session. Others need more guidance. For this latter group of students you might consider the accompanying "Brainstorming Guide." The questions on the guide can help students offer ideas on a topic.

Activity 4: Brainstorming for Ideas

Explain brainstorming to your students and then brainstorm a list of topics for writing with your class. List the topics on the board or an overhead projector. After listing several topics, divide your class into groups of four to six students. Instruct each group to select a topic and brainstorm ideas for it. Each group should choose a recorder who will write down all the ideas that are generated. If you feel that it will be helpful, distribute copies of the "Brainstorming Guide." Your students may use the worksheet for notes. Put a time limit of 10 minutes on the brainstorming. After brainstorming, while still in groups, students should review the ideas that were generated, identify

Name _____ Date _____ Class _____

Brainstorming Guide

Directions: Thinking about the following questions will help you to offer ideas during brainstorming. Write notes and ideas on this sheet.

Topic: _____

Describe your topic.

What does it do or make?

Does it influence anything? If yes, how?

Who, if anyone, is involved with it?

Is it helpful or harmful to people?

Where is it found?

Where does it come from?

Does it depend on anything?

Does it take place at a special place? Where?

Does it take place at a special time? When?

What is special about the topic?

What is important about it?

What would you like to tell others about it?

relationships, and expand the ideas. Allow about 10 minutes for this. Upon completion, each recorder or designated reporter should share his or her group's brainstormed list with the rest of the class. To conclude the activity, you may wish to have students write about their topics.

REHEARSING

It often helps to share our ideas for writing before we write. This is called rehearsing or discussing. Since the rehearsal will help students order their thoughts and generate many more ideas and angles for writing, it can be a valuable prewriting activity. This is especially true for younger or inexperienced writers, as well as students with auditory learning styles.

Rehearsing is most effective when students work with a partner. Working together, one partner assumes the role of speaker while the other listens. The speaker then shares his or her ideas for writing. The listener's responsibility is to summarize what the speaker said, ask questions about anything that seems unclear, and answer any questions the speaker may have. Hearing his or her ideas repeated may help the speaker to clarify and refine them. After the speaker has received feedback, students reverse the roles, with the speaker becoming the listener and the listener the speaker.

Activity 5: Rehearsing for Ideas

Explain to your students how rehearsing can be an effective prewriting activity. After the explanation you might wish to give them practice in rehearsing. Divide students into pairs and tell them to select a topic they would like to write about. (If you have an odd number in class, you may wish to work with a student.) Encourage students to use either clustering or idea listing to generate ideas about their topics. Allow about 10 minutes for this. Next, have them share their ideas for writing with their partner. One student acts as the speaker and the other as the listener. After the speaker is done and has received feedback, the students reverse the roles. You may find it helpful to hand out copies of the accompanying "A Prewriting Warm-up." The listeners can use the sheet as a guide to ask questions of the speaker. After this activity, students should write about their topics.

ORAL COMPOSING

Oral composing is much like rehearsing in that both are oral prewriting exercises. However, in oral composing, a story is the final product.

You can use oral composing with the entire class, divide your class into groups, or even do it one on one (which can be most effective with learning disabled students). Oral composing is a fun, relatively risk-free activity. It allows students who may be shy or have trouble getting started with writing a chance to participate. Using a tape recorder can provide additional motivation. Following are three activities that you may wish to try with your students.

A Prewriting Warm-up

Directions: Listen to your partner as he or she tells you about ideas for writing. Use the following questions to help focus your attention during listening and take notes. When your partner is done, summarize the ideas.

1. What is your partner's purpose for writing?

   _____

   _____

2. Who will the target audience be? _____

   _____

3. What is the main idea? _____

   _____

4. What are some examples? _____

   _____

   _____

   _____

   _____

5. What are some details? _____

   _____

   _____

   _____

   _____

Activity 6-1: Oral Composing—Group Stories

Divide your class into groups of four or five students. The group decides on a story to write, and students take turns composing the lines of the story. A recorder writes the sentences down. At the end of the session, the recorder reads the story first to the group and then to the class.

Activity 6-2: Oral Composing—Picture Stories

Obtain several pictures of scenes of nature. (Old calendars and magazines are good sources.) Divide your students into groups of four or five. Hand out several pictures to each group and let the group pick one that they will write a story about. Students take turns composing the lines of the story. A recorder writes down the story and reads it back to the group and the class. As a follow-up, students may select pictures of their own and write their own stories. (Fine art postcards and feature photography in newspapers or magazines also work well for this.)

Activity 6-3: Oral Composing—Story Starters

Divide your students into groups of four or five. Read one (or both, if you wish to give your students a choice) of the story starters to the group. Each student takes a turn and adds a sentence to the story. A recorder writes the sentences down and later reads the completed story.

- He saw the answer key to the history test on the floor. It must have fallen out of Mrs. Martin's book. No one was around. He needed an "A" on the test tomorrow . . .

- It was dark by the time she left school. She did not like walking home alone like this, but she had no choice. She walked quickly, being careful to stay away from shadows. The sound startled her . . .

ROLE-PLAYING

Role-playing is yet another prewriting activity. It is especially useful for generating ideas, dialogue, or information or when students are writing stories and must detail the feelings and actions of characters. Role-playing can help young writers create believable characters.

Frequently students are hesitant to utilize role-playing. They may feel uncomfortable, or they may not know how to begin. An easy way to start a role-playing session is to have students role-play familiar people in very limited situations. Ask someone to role-play a parent, brother, or sister. Or you might suggest role-playing an actor or actress in a favorite scene.

Activity 7: Role-Playing to Find Ideas

Explain to your students how role-playing can be a valuable prewriting strategy. After the explanation, you may like to run the following activity to give your students practice in role-playing. Divide your class into groups of four or five. Make sure that

Choose a Role

Directions: Choose a scene and role-play the characters with the members of your group.

- You are shopping at the mall with some of your friends. On the way home, one of your friends reveals the gold chain he or she shoplifted. With the members of your group, role-play what you would do next.

- You and a friend are home alone at night, studying upstairs for a big science test. You hear a noise at one of the downstairs back windows. With a partner acting as your friend, role-play what you do next.

- You and a friend rode your bikes to a local convenience store to buy sodas. When you come out, one of the bikes is gone. With a partner, role-play what you would do.

- You did not do your homework. You know that your teacher will be angry and will likely call your parent who will ground you for the big dance. With a partner playing the teacher, role-play your explanation to your teacher why you didn't have your homework.

- You are applying for a summer job that you want very much. You must convince the boss why you are the person he or she should hire. With a partner acting as the boss, role-play how you would handle this important meeting.

Design your own. With the members of your group, brainstorm some situations for role-playing. Select parts and role-play the characters.

there is enough room between the groups so that students will have space in which to act out their roles. Ask them to think of a role they would like to play. They should consider the person they will be playing in a particular situation. A good example is two friends who are walking home from school and find a lost wallet. Students could role-play what the friends do next. Ideally, the situations and roles students choose should include other members of the group. Having at least two people involved in a role-play helps to uncover more ideas because of the interaction. Every member of the group should do at least one role-play.

If you wish, you can hand out copies of the accompanying "Choose a Role," which offers several suggestions for role-playing. After the practice role-playing is done, suggest that students think of something important that happened to them, explain it to the group, and then, with partners, role-play it. They may like to write about this event in their journals.

RESEARCHING

Researching is another prewriting activity. After a writer has selected a topic and identified general ideas, frequently he or she must gather additional information. While much of the writing done in writing workshop will not require outside research, students should realize that many writing projects do need to be researched.

Activity 8: Researching

This activity is best implemented when students are actually involved in researching a topic for writing. Explain to your students that before beginning research, they should make a plan. After deciding on a topic, they should read general background information on it. Not only will this help them to formulate questions about their topics, it will help them to focus their ideas and direct their research efforts.

The first place many students go for research is the encyclopedia. Explain that although references like encyclopedias can provide general information, students should consult specific books on their topics. They can find these books through the card catalog of their school or public library. (If some of your students need help in using a card catalog, set up library time and present a separate lesson on it.)

Taking notes is an essential researching skill. I allow students to use either note cards or ordinary paper. I suggest that they use only one side of each card or paper for notes and put only one topic on each, because this makes it easier to organize later. I also require students to include full bibliographical data for each source on each sheet (author, title, place of publication, publisher, date, and pages). Not only does this make it easier to go back to the source if facts need to be rechecked, but it also makes compiling a complete bibliography simpler.

In taking their notes, emphasize to students to record only essential information. To make that task easier, suggest that students ask themselves the same questions reporters ask when doing an article—who, what, where, when, why, and how. By asking themselves these questions as they conduct their research, they are more likely to zero in on the most important information.

ORGANIZING WRITING

Effective organization helps authors to write clearly and express exactly what they want to say. This is especially important for assigned topics such as research papers. Organization can take many forms from standard outlines to simple sequence lists. The accompanying "A Structure Form" can help students organize ideas. Note, however, that some form of freer prewriting should usually precede this. Be sure that methods of organization never overwhelm students, making the students worry more about the method than the writing. Organizational strategies should aid and never inhibit writing.

Outlines or structure lists are helpful because they enable the author to think through his or her piece before the actual writing. Tell your students it is a bit like a rehearsal. They can identify main ideas and details, sequence material, cut and paste, and map out the general direction they wish to go with their writing. Emphasize that changes and adjustments will be made during drafting and that the basic outline should never be thought to provide more than general guidance.

DRAWING AND DIAGRAMMING

Although most students will not rely on drawing and diagramming as prewriting activities, a few will. Sometimes these students have artistic ability and feel at ease using drawings and diagrams as part of their efforts to explore ideas. Occasionally, you will have students who simply find that sketching can help them uncover ideas and insights. One particularly helpful prewriting method here is storyboarding, in which ideas are sequenced in picture form. Flowcharting is another. Often, artwork can be used to enhance the final written piece.

JOURNALS

Writing journals contain an author's ideas, questions, visions, dreams, and anything in between. Journals are usually written in the first person and may explore a variety of topics. Sometimes the topics may be personal; sometimes they may be general. Journals permit students to experiment with new writing forms, help establish the habit of writing, and enable students to witness their growth as writers. Journals also become repositories of ideas for writing.

As the teacher, you must decide on the rules regarding journals. Will they be private? Will you look at them? Will they be shared? And if they will, with whom? Once set, these rules should never be violated. If they are, trust will be undermined, and some students may become reluctant to write. You may wish to hand out the accompanying "Writing Journal Guidelines for Students" and discuss its points in a mini-lesson.

I recommend reviewing the journals of students periodically. This allows you the opportunity to respond to their writing and helps ensure that all students write in their journals regularly. While some teachers prefer to collect the journals of their students at set intervals—every two weeks, for example—others prefer to read a few from each

Name _____ Date _____ Class _____

A Structure Form

Main idea: _____

    Detail: _____

    Detail: _____

    Detail: _____

Main idea: _____

    Detail: _____

    Detail: _____

    Detail: _____

Main idea: _____

    Detail: _____

    Detail: _____

    Detail: _____

Main idea: _____

    Detail: _____

    Detail: _____

    Detail: _____

Writing Journal
Guidelines for Students

1. Use a standard, spiral notebook for your journal. When you run out of space, continue your journal in another notebook. Number your journals.

2. Use your journal only for writing. Do not use it for other subjects.

3. Write in your journal outside as well as during writing workshop. Write in it whenever you have something to record or reflect on.

4. Write about topics that interest you. They can be real or fiction.

5. Experiment with new writing forms and styles in your journal.

6. Be alert that I will read your journal periodically. While I will not grade your writing, I will offer comments and suggestions. Feel free to write back to me in your journal. We can carry on a dialogue.

7. For those entries you do not want me to read, fold over the page and write across it, "Don't read." I will respect your privacy, but remember that if I read something that I feel endangers you or someone else, I must report it.

8. Take some of your good journal entries and develop them into polished pieces.

9. Share what you feel are your best entries with the class.

10. Review your journal periodically and see how you are growing as a writer.

Some possible topics:

My Family	My Values	Worrying
Being the Youngest	Being the Oldest	Being Dumped
Changes in Me	Friendship	Home
Time of Happiness	Time of Sadness	Hobbies

class two or three times a week. I still get to read everyone's journal at least once every two weeks or so, but I find that this schedule makes the work load manageable.

To assure students of their privacy, you may instruct them to fold down any pages of their journals that they do not want you to read. In this way students feel free to include personal thoughts in their journals. However, you should tell them that if you read something in a journal that leads you to believe someone is in danger, you are obligated to report it.

While you should not grade or correct the writing in journals—only finished pieces should be used for grading—you should comment on your students' writing. Offer suggestions, constructive remarks, questions, and encouragement whenever possible. Sometimes students will respond to the teacher's comments, and they and the teacher will carry on a correspondence through the journals.

One of the biggest problems with writing journals is that some students use them simply as a way to record the day's events. They slip into the routine of writing diary entries without reflection or real purpose. You can reduce this by encouraging your students to write about a variety of topics and take what they feel are the better entries and develop them into finished pieces.

Journals offer students the opportunity to reflect on their world and expand their awareness of what is happening in their lives. For many students journals become a rich source of ideas for writing.

IDEA FOLDERS

Idea folders are containers for ideas. In this, they are similar to journals. You can use ordinary manila folders or big envelopes (9" by 12" is a good size) or have students make folders from oak tag or construction paper. Idea folders are the place to put clippings from newspapers or magazines, questions that don't get entered into their journals, or anything else that can be an idea for further reflection or future writing.

Some teachers prefer only to suggest to students that they keep idea folders, while others require them. If you decide to require them, keep them in boxes in your classroom. Label the boxes by class, and file the folders alphabetically according to the students' last names. Make the box of idea folders available for the class and allow your students to go to the folders as necessary.

Remind your students to go through their idea folders periodically as a type of house cleaning. Idea folders can be most valuable on those occasions when students are having trouble finding a topic for writing.

I keep an idea folder, too. It's an old box that once held envelopes. Anything that I feel might one day be an idea for writing gets dropped into the box. While most of the tidbits don't amount to anything, a few do. They justify the effort. If you decide to use idea folders in your classroom, you should discuss their setup and benefits with your students.

PERSONAL EXPERIENCE

One of the best places to find ideas for writing is in personal experiences. Things that happen to us, or things that we have learned of, can often spark an idea.

Activity 9: Personal Experience and Ideas

Discuss the importance of personal experience to one's writing. Explain to your students that it is likely that they have already had many experiences that could provide fine material for writing, but that they just have not uncovered them. Tell them that good ideas for writing are often hidden and tucked away in ordinary events. We have to search for them to bring them out. A helpful plan is to take a personal inventory of their experiences. The accompanying "Inventory of Personal Experience" can help students identify possible topics for writing. Hand out copies to your students and encourage them to answer the questions in their journals. They can write as much or as little about each question as they like. Not all the questions need to be answered during one period.

You may find students who will look at the list of questions and find an idea for writing immediately. Others will answer several questions before finding a topic. Any questions they do answer, however, should go into their journals for later use. Whenever students become stumped for a topic during writing workshop, suggest that they check their journals for ideas.

OBSERVATION

The world is an interesting place, and it is full of ideas for writing. Encourage your students to become keen observers of their world. They should learn to see things not in isolation, but in relation to other things. How do things affect each other? How are they connected? Encourage your students to use all their senses—seeing, hearing, touching, smelling, and tasting—to gain full appreciation of their world.

Activity 10: Observation and Ideas

Explain to your students how observation can be important to prewriting. Offer them this example. Most people see a tree only as a trunk, branches, and leaves. It's much more. Its roots hold the soil and draw water from the ground. It provides a home for birds, squirrels, and other animals. Its leaves are food and shelter for insects. Trees help provide the world's atmospheric oxygen. Every tree is a part of an ecosystem, and each of these relationships can be a possible topic for writing.

As a follow-up to your explanation, you may wish to assign this activity. Ask your students to choose a place—a park, backyard, their rooms are some examples. They are to stay at the place they select for 15 minutes to a half-hour and observe the spot. What is there? What are the relationships? How is each of their senses affected? To help your students with their observations, you can hand out copies of "What Do You See?" which is included. Encourage your students to write about their observations in their journals.

ANGLES AND VIEWPOINTS

In their search for ideas and topics for writing, encourage your students to view things from various angles and viewpoints. There are several sides to an issue. While

Name _____ Date _____ Class _____

Inventory of Personal Experience

Directions: Answer the following questions in your journal. Write as much or as little as you wish about each question. Reviewing your answers from time to time will help you to generate ideas for writing.

What am I interested in?

What things do I especially like? What things do I dislike?

What makes me different from other people?

What do I like about myself? What do I dislike?

What would I change about myself?

What makes me feel good about myself?

What do I care about most?

What would I most like to know?

What would I like to do?

Where would I like to go?

What exciting things have I done?

Do I know any interesting people? Why are they interesting?

What could I share with others?

What would I like to change about the world?

What are some things that have made me happy?

What are some things that have made me sad?

What are some things that have made me angry?

What are some things that have made me afraid?

What advice or insight could I share with others?

What Do You See?

Directions: Choose a place to observe. Some examples include a park, backyard, a main street, even a shopping mall. Stay at this place for 15 to 30 minutes and observe what happens. Answering the following questions will help focus your observation. Use the back of this sheet if you need more space. You may wish to write about your observation in your journal.

1. What is the place you selected to observe? _____

_____

2. Describe this place._____

_____

_____

3. What relationships do you see? _____

_____

4. What do you smell? _____

_____

5. What do you hear? _____

_____

6. Can you touch anything? _____ What do these things feel like? _____

_____

7. Can you taste anything? _____ How do these things taste? _____

_____

light contains the colors of the rainbow, those colors are rarely seen. Few issues come in simple black or white; most have several shades between extremes. Teach your students to look for those shades.

Activity 11: Angles and Viewpoints

Explain to your students how excellent ideas for writing can be obtained by viewing things from various angles. When most people agree on an issue, tell your students to look at those who disagree. Why do they disagree? What do they see that others do not? Why do they feel the way they do? Tell your students to look at things from the back, side, top, and bottom. Everybody knows what it looks like from the front.

To help your students gain an appreciation of varying viewpoints, try this activity. Divide your class into groups of four to six. Ask them to consider this statement— "Parents have the right to search their children's rooms." Working in their groups, students are to discuss the statement. Each group should select a recorder who is to write down the major ideas the group discusses. Instruct your students to consider the issue from their point of view as well as the position of parents. Why might parents search a child's room? What might they be worried about? Is such an act ever justified? What about the feelings of the child? Does the child have a right to absolute privacy? To aid students with their discussion, you can distribute copies of "Seeing All Sides." Allow students 10 to 15 minutes to discuss the topic. After the discussion, have each recorder report to the class the major ideas the group discussed. After each recorder has shared his or her group's discussion, you should point out how many different ideas and opinions have been shared, and how one usually leads to others. Before ending the class, be sure to note some of the ideas that can probably be developed into topics for writing.

USING QUESTIONS TO EXPLORE TOPICS

Once students find topics for writing, many have trouble developing them. They lack the skill to examine their subjects so that they gain a full understanding of them. Many good topics for writing are lost because of this.

First, students should consider the scope of their subjects. Some topics are broad and connect with other topics. What are the areas of overlap? Finding those areas can often help students zero in on fresh angles for writing. It is not uncommon for students to start with a topic, and then, as they explore that topic, find a better one to write about.

Focusing on a topic that is narrow enough for writing is essential. Unfortunately, this is a step that many students resist. You must constantly remind them how important this is. Tell them to look for the most interesting aspect of a topic. What excites them about it? What would others like to know about it?

Students should also consider their target audience. Who are they writing for? They may be writing for other students, parents, or the public. Knowing their target audience enables them to gear their writing for that particular group.

When considering nonfiction writing topics, the most basic questions to answer are the five W's and how:

Seeing All Sides

Directions: Think about this statement—"Parents have the right to search their children's rooms." First consider it from the point of view of a student; then imagine being a parent. How might a parent react to the statement? Answering the questions below will help you to see both sides of the issue. After completing the worksheet, you might like to explore this topic further and write about it in your journal.

1. Do parents ever have the right to search a child's room? If yes, when? If no, why not?

Student Answer: _____

_____

Parent Answer: _____

_____

2. What might a parent's reasons be for searching a child's room?

Student Answer: _____

_____

Parent Answer: _____

_____

3. Does the fact that a child is a minor in the parent's home give parents a right to search? Why or why not?

Student Answer: _____

_____

Parent Answer: _____

_____

- What is the subject?
- Who is involved?
- When did/does this happen?
- Where did/does it happen?
- Why did/does it happen?
- How did/does it happen?

These questions can help students to understand their topics in a general way. But there is more. Students should go beyond the five W's and how. The various prewriting strategies dicussed earlier are effective in helping students to elaborate on their topics.

Activity 12: Focusing Topics

Explain to your students the importance of focusing their topics before writing. Stress the need to narrow down their topic and also the value of recognizing how the topic is linked to others. The points of connection can often provide unique insight to the topic. Discuss the target audience, too. Knowing for whom he or she is writing enables an author to tailor the work for that particular reader. Finally, talk about the five W's and how, but note that good writers go beyond these questions. They ask even more. As an example of some of these questions, distribute copies of "Exploring a Writing Topic." Review it with your students and encourage them to use it when they develop topics for writing.

There are many methods that writers use to find and develop ideas. Introduce as many of the prewriting techniques as you can and encourage your students to use the ones they feel are most helpful.

Exploring a Writing Topic

Directions: Whenever you are thinking about a topic for writing, consider the following:

1. Think of the big picture. How broad is my topic?

2. Where does my topic overlap or touch others? (Points of overlap can be good topics for writing.)

3. Use the "5 W's" and "how" to define your topic. (What? Who? When? Where? Why? How?)

4. Once you understand the broad topic, narrow it down. What exactly do you want to write about?

5. After focusing your topic, examine it again. What are the parts now? Can it be narrowed further?

6. What is the history of your topic? Where did it come from?

7. What is its purpose?

8. What does it affect? How does it affect other things?

9. How is it influenced by other things?

10. What will your topic be like in the future? How will it change?

11. Why is the topic important?

12. Why am I interested in the topic?

13. What is my purpose in writing about this topic?

14. Who will my audience be?

15. What do I want to tell them about this topic?

4

Drafting

Drafting is the stage of the writing process when ideas are shaped and expressed on paper. After drafting begins, the author moves back and forth through composing, reviewing, and revising his draft until he stops.

The author reaches the drafting stage when he moves from prewriting to the actual writing of the piece. Like the rest of the parts of drafting, the beginning may be fast, a rush from prewriting to composing carried by great energy, or it may be slow, filled with hesitation and rethinking. Perhaps the writer is not sure of his lead paragraph; maybe he is uncertain how best to support a main idea in the opening paragraph, or he might not know how to sequence his ideas.

The composing part of the drafting stage is filled with periods of slow and fast writing, interspersed with pauses. As the writer works, ideas are expanded, clarified, and reformulated. The author is deeply involved with the piece.

While he writes, the author will frequently review what he has written. He may reread his work; reconsider the sequence of ideas; reflect on the lead, the conclusion, or the development; or decide to change details. Composing thus often overlaps with revision. (This should not be confused with the final revision stage of the writing process, when authors revise the finished draft.)

Some students will complete their drafts with only one or two pauses, while others will revise heavily, agonizing over using just the right word. Urge your students to write their drafts without concern for revision, because some will worry so much about writing perfectly on their drafts that they will be barely able to write at all! Especially, urge them to avoid time-consuming techniques like whiting out. However, you should not force those who feel that they must revise as they go along to abandon writing the way they feel most comfortable (as long as they remain productive).

The final part of drafting is the stopping point. The writer has finished the draft and now is ready to begin the next stage of the writing process—revision. Of course that may lead back to drafting, and students may produce one, two, three, or more drafts of the same piece.

It is important to realize that your students will work at different rates as they do their drafts. Some will write their drafts in one sitting, their imaginations entirely involved, while others will work in spurts. Some will splash ideas onto the paper like painters and others will reveal ideas slowly, as if never certain that the thought they are expressing is the right one.

Encourage—and demand, if necessary—that your students complete their drafts. Every draft that is finished is a milestone. While the work of revision is just beginning, the major effort of completing the piece has been accomplished.

Activity 13: The Stages of Drafting

Explain the parts of the drafting stage: starting, composing, reviewing, revising, and stopping. Be sure to mention how students are likely to shift back and forth through the parts. When students understand that other writers go through the same steps in creating their drafts, they no longer feel alone in their efforts to produce good work. Knowing that other writers feel and do what they do will give them encouragement.

Activity 14: Questions to Ask During Drafting

Students who plan their drafts usually find writing easier than do those who simply begin writing. Explain that by asking themselves questions like the following as they write, they will be able to keep their thoughts focused.

- What is my purpose for writing?

- What will my audience want to know about my topic?

- What do I want to say?

- How can I best arrange my information?

- What are my main ideas?

- What details can I use to support my main ideas?

- What will make a good lead?

- What will make a strong conclusion?

*THE FOUNDATIONS OF GOOD WRITING*_____

Being aware of the elements of good writing can help students as they work on their drafts. While the types of writing and forms of expression vary, all good writing shares common foundations.

Good writing is interesting. The words and ideas draw readers into what the writer is saying. The writer knows her audience and tailors her work so that her readers will feel a kinship with her. The audience will understand her even if they don't always agree with what she is saying.

Good writing is simple and concise. The prose is tight and ideas are expressed clearly. Unnecessary words, sentences, paragraphs, and pages have been eliminated.

Good writing reflects the clear thinking of its author. The author has examined her material, considered its arrangement, and communicates exactly what she wants to say.

Good writing exhibits freshness. Its style flows naturally out of the author's experiences and perceptions. It is free of redundancies and clichés and, instead, relies on strong imagery to paint pictures for the readers. Its descriptions are precise and colorful, exciting the senses so that the reader is transported, through imagination, to the scene the author is sharing.

Finally, good writing employs correct mechanics. Mistakes in punctuation, grammar, spelling, and usage undermine writing and obscure ideas. They can ruin what otherwise might be a fine piece.

Activity 15: The Foundations of Good Writing

Discuss the foundations of good writing with your students. Encourage them to recall the following points when they are writing:

- *Good writing* is aimed at a specific audience.

- *Good writing* is interesting.

- *Good writing* is simple and concise.

- *Good writing* reflects the clear thinking of its author.

- *Good writing* is fresh.

- *Good writing* has strong imagery.

- *Good writing* has correct punctuation, grammar, spelling, and word usage.

STRATEGIES TO AID DRAFTING

Some students find drafting to be the hardest stage of the writing process. The ideas that have been generated during prewriting must now be written in an organized fashion. That can be a frightening prospect.

There are several strategies you can employ to help your students with their drafts. First, remember that every student is an individual. Your students will write at different paces. Avoid breaking your writing schedule down into a tight regimen, in which everyone must be done with his or her draft on the same day. Some students will be done before that, while others will need more time. Although deadlines are appropriate to ensure that everyone completes drafts, they should be liberal enough to allow for individual working styles.

You will undoubtedly have students who say that they don't know how to start their drafts. When you ask them for some possible openings, they may have nothing to offer. For these students you may have to suggest that they simply begin writing about their topics, which will engage their minds and warm them to the task of composing.

As your students compose, refrain from interrupting them. Let them work. Interruptions—even a pat on the back—at this point can cause good ideas to be lost.

Circulate around the room and help students who have questions or who are blocked. If a student is having trouble clarifying ideas, you might encourage him to tell you orally what he is trying to write. If he is having trouble deciding on a lead, you might ask him what kinds of leads he is considering and ask him to share with you what he feels are the strengths and weaknesses of each. If a student is having trouble with sequence, you might suggest that he list his ideas in order of importance.

Because they lack confidence, some students will ask you what they should do. Offer suggestions, but encourage them to make decisions. Emphasize that the writing is theirs and they must decide how it will be.

Sometimes during their drafting, you will need to help students focus ideas. Asking questions like: "Can you tell me more of how you'd like to develop this?" or "Can you add some description here?" will help young writers over a rough spot.

When students get blocked, you might suggest that they work with a partner or peer group and explain what they are trying to say. Sometimes just talking about their writing can help students sort their ideas enough to resume work. At other times, the partner or peers can provide the support that can help the writer move forward.

Since mechanics can be corrected during editing, they are not a priority during drafting. Tell your students to concentrate on their writing. The important thing when working on a draft is to keep fully involved with the writing. For example, students may feel that they must stop writing to consult a thesaurus to find a precise word in an expression. Suggest that this can be done during revision. Sometimes students stop writing to check a dictionary for the correct spelling of a word. I remember one boy, whose mother had told him to look up words he didn't know how to spell, who stopped repeatedly while writing his draft to check if he was spelling words correctly. He was so concerned about spelling that he had trouble writing. To help him maintain a flow of thoughts, I suggested that he simply sound out the words he was unsure of and keep writing. Spelling could be checked later. The same advice is valid for questions regarding punctuation and grammar. All can be checked and corrected during editing.

When students worry about mechanics while writing their drafts, they become anxious about making mistakes and are distracted from communicating their ideas. Their writing becomes slow; enthusiasm and energy vanish. Instead of focusing on expression, unity, logic, and development, they worry about periods and commas. As your students become more skilled in writing, they will become more aware of mechanics. Moreover, the skills of mechanics that you teach during mini-lessons and conferences will begin to be internalized.

Activity 16: Writing with Emotion on the Draft

Explain to your students that the purpose of the draft is to get their ideas down on paper. Emphasize that when drafting, they should focus on the actual writing of their piece. They should write with emotion. Mechanics at this time are secondary. Emphasize that worrying about mechanics now can undermine their writing by stealing their concentration from their work. Mechanics can be corrected later. Few professional writers complete drafts that become final copies. Most revise and edit their work many times before it is published.

Students are often reluctant to do a draft because they must commit their ideas to paper in an organized manner. To some, filling that blank sheet can seem impossible. Sometimes you may have to suggest that students begin writing whatever comes to mind about their topics in an effort to start ideas flowing. For most students, once they begin the draft, the writing comes easier.

Encourage your students to finish every draft they begin. Although revision, editing, and publishing remain to be done, the completion of the draft is in itself an accomplishment.

5

Revision

Revision is the stage of the writing process in which students "re-see" their work. Although some revision may occur during drafting, the best time for revision is after the draft has been completed. Students can then look at their drafts as whole pieces.

Revision includes adding to, deleting from, reshaping and polishing the writing of the draft, as well as making sure that what has been said is clear and is precisely what the writer intended. Revision should always be selective and focused, concentrating on those areas that need work and leaving the rest of the draft alone.

THE MECHANICS OF REVISION

When you begin teaching revision, you may find that your students don't know the mechanics of how to revise their drafts—the simple ways to add and delete information. And you may find that some students are reluctant to make any changes, because their previous teachers corrected and revised their papers for them. After red-penciling, these students would recopy their drafts and hand in final copies, the only changes being the ones made by their teachers.

To revise their work efficiently, students must understand how to make changes. Carets (∧) can be used for inserting words, phrases, or sentences. Deletions can be made by simply crossing out material, and arrows can be used to connect different parts of writing. Cutting and pasting, stapling, and stick-ons are useful for changing order and making additions. A list of editor's marks (see Activity 23) contains symbols students may use in revising their work.

Activity 17: The Mechanics of Revision

Explain the mechanics of revision to your students: how carets can be used for insertions, how material can be deleted by crossing out, and how arrows can be used

The Mechanics of Revision

Bringing a Puppy Home

There are few things as demanding as raising a puppy. But there are few things as rewarding either. ~~Puppies can bring a great deal of joy to your house, but a lot of work, too~~

When you bring your puppy home, you should do all you can to reduce his stress. Remember, the puppy has just been separated from his mother and littermates.

He is probably frightened. ~~You should~~ show him kindness and attention but ~~not too much~~ Don't tire him out. That will only make his adjustment harder. You should have a place for your puppy to stay. Dogs are den animals ~~by nature~~ They desire a small place of their own, Like a wooden crate or a box. You should put a blanket or some carpeting in there for him, And you should keep it clean. Your puppy will come to like his home.

It is important that you feed your puppy a healthy diet. You should check with the person you bought him from to find out what he has been eating. Continuing that diet will prevent digestion problems. If you decide to change his food, do it gradually, mixing new food with his old.

One of your ~~first~~ responsibilities is to take your puppy to a veterinarian for an examination. ~~He~~ *your puppy* must have shots to protect him from diseases like rabies and distemper. Your vet can also advise you about ~~his~~ *your puppy's* diet and answer any questions about his health that you may have.

Raising a puppy is a big responsibility. But if you do a good job you will have a fine companion for many years to come.

to connect the sections of a piece. Also mention the advantages of cutting and pasting and stick-ons. You may wish to distribute copies of the accompanying "The Mechanics of Revision" to show your students an example of a draft.

Discuss the paragraph with your students and point out why the revisions were made. For example, point out that the title was changed. The third sentence of the first paragraph was deleted because it was redundant—it said the same thing as the first two sentences. Note the change in the second paragraph and also that "not too much" is unnecessary to the writer's intention. In the revised third paragraph that begins with "You should," "by nature" is unnecessary, the fragment is corrected, and connecting the two sentences helps the writing to flow more smoothly. In the fifth paragraph, one may wonder why a "first" responsibility would be placed at the end of the piece. Also in that paragraph, the change to "your puppy" reduces the chance that the reader might mistakenly think that the vet needs the shots or that his diet is being discussed. Finally, a conclusion is added.

If you want to take this lesson a little further, ask students if the piece addresses every question they would have about raising puppies. (They might suggest adding sections on housebreaking or training.)

TEACHING REVISION

Since most students lack the skills to revise their writing, you must offer direction. I start by telling my students that almost all writers revise their work; few manage to write exactly what they wish the first time. Good writing is a result of good revision. Next, I suggest that before making any changes students read their entire drafts to get a feeling for the scope and flow. Sometimes reading their drafts out loud is helpful because they can hear the rhythm of their words. Finally, I tell my students to concentrate on the essential characteristics of good writing: unity, order, and conciseness. As they become more skilled at revision, I add more elements, which I draw from the mini-lessons of Part II of this book.

REVISING FOR UNITY AND ORDER

In reading for unity (or "focus"), students should determine if their words, phrases, and sentences build to a single purpose. Is there a common line that ties everything together? A piece about soccer, for example, should remain focused on soccer and not digress to baseball. A unified piece has a clear opening, solid development, and strong conclusion. Main ideas are supported with details, but the details do not overshadow the ideas they support. The style should also be consistent and appropriate for the piece. A lighthearted style would not be proper for a serious piece, and while a straightforward style might work for an informational article, it may not be a good choice for a horror short story. In a unified piece, everything draws together to give the author's main idea clarity and impact.

Order addresses logic and form. As students reread their pieces, tell them to examine its development. Does each sentence and idea logically follow the one before it? Does the piece progress from a beginning to conclusion? Are the facts valid and presented consistently? Is the author's point getting across? Young authors often assume that readers know what the author is saying even when the author fails to say it.

REVISING FOR CONCISENESS

Conciseness is vital for clarity. When pieces become cluttered with unnecessary material in which several words are used where one or two are sufficient, ideas become obscure. The writing also becomes boring. Here are some cluttered sentences that can easily be made more concise:

The horse's nature was gentle.
The horse was gentle.

The fox came up to the rabbit in a sly manner.
The fox crept up on the rabbit. (Note that the stronger verb "crept" eliminates the need for the adverb.)

Conciseness is also compromised by redundancy. A good example is the phrase "serious danger." A dangerous condition *is* serious. Another is the phrase "he thought to himself." To whom else *could* he think? Redundancies are easy to revise. The offending word or words are simply eliminated. (See Mini-lesson 20, "Conciseness," of Part II.)

PITFALLS TO AVOID

Your students will often ask you how they should revise their writing. While you may offer options, resist making the revisions yourself, since this relieves the student of the responsibility for reworking and polishing his ideas and slows his growth as a writer.

You should also be cautious of using labels like "awkward," "vague," or "illogical" when referring to the writing of your students. If they don't understand the meanings of such words, they will not know how to correct their mistakes. While you should be cautious in using negatives, you should discuss writing with your students using words authors use. For example, refer to the beginning of an article as the lead, and its ending as the conclusion. In a story the resolution occurs in the climax. Using correct terminology promotes understanding and helps students to see themselves as authors.

Activity 18: A Revision Plan

The following steps provide a plan that students can follow when they approach revision. Start out by explaining that virtually every author revises his or her work. As writers become more skilled in revision, they develop their own procedures because revision is as much art as it is craft. No two authors revise in the same way. Until your students become comfortable with their own methods for revision, they will likely find it helpful to follow a plan.

1. Read the piece silently and then aloud. Reading it aloud can highlight the flow and rhythm of the words.

2. Consider the whole piece first. What are its strengths? What parts do you like the best? What are its weaknesses? How can the weaknesses be improved? What can be added? What can be eliminated?

3. Next, focus on the paragraphs. Are they well organized? Does each have a main idea that is supported by details? Do the paragraphs follow each other logically? Are the transitions between them smooth?

4. Now consider the sentences. Do they follow each other logically? Are they clear?

5. Focus on the words and phrases. Which should be changed? Which are examples of clutter?

WRITING CONFERENCES

A writing conference occurs when a student meets with you or with another student or students about writing. Conferences need not be formal or lengthy. Some may last only a minute or two. They may take place at the student's desk, a writing table, the teacher's desk, or even on the floor.

The purpose of conferences is to help students improve their writing. You might listen to a student read her opening in an effort to make it stronger, help another student focus his topic, or suggest ways a student can improve imagery. Through conferences you can share tips for better writing, help students learn the techniques of revision, and reinforce the skills you taught during mini-lessons. You can also uncover common problems students are having in your class and address those problems via mini-lessons.

No matter where you meet, how long the conference lasts, or what it is about, successful writing conferences share the same characteristics. Most important, they are focused. You must address only one or two points in the conference. More than that will overwhelm your students, making it hard for them to accomplish the necessary changes. Successful conferences require an atmosphere of support and cooperation, so that you and your students will feel comfortable enough in the conference setting to ask questions and discuss how their writing can be improved. Finally, successful conferences help students to read and evaluate their work critically, leading to the growth of writing skills.

I suggest that you move around the room and go to your students for conferences. I find that when I stay at my desk, students line up for help. Not only do some begin "fooling around," but valuable writing time is lost as they wait. By circulating, you avoid the lines. Moreover, when you move around the room, it is easier to monitor the behavior and progress of your students.

Many conferences will begin with students offering you a question or problem. However, you will have to initiate conferences with others. You might start a conference by asking, "How are you doing with this?" If a student simply says okay, ask him to read some of his piece to you. You may then respond to the writing. If a student does not need help, let him work and move on to another.

Activity 19: A Role-Played Writing Conference

When most students don't know what to expect in a writing conference, I role-play a conference for the class. (If your students have experience with the writing workshop format, this activity may not be necessary.) I try to do this early in the school year. Select a student to play the part of the student. You will be the teacher. Set up a desk or a table at a section of the room. The role-playing begins with the student working on a piece. You approach, then the two of you act out the script that is provided. You might wish to make copies so that you and the student can read from it. (Note that there are two scripts, one in which you begin the conference and the other in which the student initiates the meeting.) At the end of the role-playing, point out to your students that you will offer guidance during conferences, but that they must retain the ownership of their pieces; that is, the writing must be theirs, not yours.

You will encounter various situations and problems during conferences with your students. Most will require guidance or a gentle nudge to help the student around an obstacle that is blocking her. Frequently, the key is in asking questions that can get the student thinking about solutions to the problem. "Who's your audience?" "What are you trying to get across here?" "What do you want the reader to think about this?" "What are the possibilities from this point?" "What's your favorite part?" "What's the most troublesome part?" These and similar questions can help young authors around problems that can block their way to finishing a satisfying piece.

When a student asks a question about her writing, you may offer suggestions or alternatives but leave the decision to her. Letting her find her own answer is the best way of learning. It is vital that you do not tell your student what to do or how to revise. Once you begin making decisions, you take ownership of the piece. It no longer belongs fully to the writer, and once that happens motivation is undermined. Why should a student work as hard on a piece that isn't hers anymore?

When you ask questions, make them open-ended: "What's your main point?" "What do you want to tell us about the house?" "How would you describe the storm?"

SOME CONFERENCE STRATEGIES

Following are some typical writing problems and questions you might consider asking. As you pose questions to your students, they will begin to ask those same questions to themselves and each other. They will become more aware of writing and become their own evaluators. (They will also eventually become more critical readers of published writing.)

Conference problem:	The topic is too broad.
Teacher's questions:	What's the most important idea in your piece? What is your purpose in writing this? What's the most interesting part of this piece?
Conference problem:	The writing lacks information.
Teacher's questions:	What more can you tell me about your topic? What else might the reader want to know?
Conference problem:	There is no opening.
Teacher's questions:	How can you lead into your story? How can you "hook" the reader?

A Writing Conference
Started by the Teacher

Teacher: How are you doing?

Student: OK.

T. (sits down by student): Where are you on this?

S. (frowns): After the opening.

T. How can I help?

S. (hesitates): I'm stuck.

T. You mean you don't know where to go next?

S. (nods): Yeah.

T. Can you read it to me?

S. All right. (begins reading) I moved from New York City last year to _____. I didn't want to move. I didn't like our new home. (looks at teacher)

T. I think you started out fine, but now I'd like to know more. Could you tell me why you didn't want to move? And why didn't you like your new home?

A Writing Conference
Started by a Student

(Student is seated at a desk and raises hand.)

Teacher (approaches student): How can I help, _____?

Student: I'm writing an essay, but I'm not sure about the sequence.

T. How did you arrange your information?

S. I just took my ideas and wrote them down.

T. What don't you like about the way it turned out?

S. Well, it just doesn't sound right.

T. Can you read what you have for me?

S. (begins reading from paper) Recycling is an important way to conserve the Earth's resources. When we recycle, we take materials that were used before and change them so that we can use them again. We can recycle paper, glass, plastic, steel, and aluminum. Recycling helps to save landfill space. It also helps to save energy.

T. Umm . . . you have a lot of good facts there, but I agree you could arrange them better. Try thinking of ways you might reorder the sentences in that paragraph.

S. (thinks a few moments) What about moving the last two sentences to the beginning of the paragraph? They follow the idea of the Earth's resources.

T. That's a possibility. Why don't you try that?

Conference problem:	There is no conclusion.
Teacher's questions:	How can you end your piece? Is this a satisfying ending? Does the conclusion help your reader get your main point?
Conference problem:	The writing lacks organization.
Teacher's questions:	How can you order your ideas to make them clearer? Are some ideas more important than others? Would a sequence of some kind make sense here?
Conference problem:	The writing lacks unity.
Teacher's questions:	Do all your ideas fit your purpose? What is your main focus?
Conference problem:	The writing is bland and colorless.
Teacher's questions:	Can you tell me what it would be like if I were there? What would my senses tell me? What are some interesting details you could add to this?
Conference problem:	The writing uses too much description or lacks conciseness.
Teacher's questions:	How can you make your writing tighter? Are you worried about length? (Some students will admit to padding.)
Conference problem:	The writer relies on passive rather than active voice.
Teacher's questions:	What stronger action verbs can you use? Do you know the difference between active and passive constructions? (You may have to give a quick lesson.)

PEER CONFERENCES

Peer conferences are one way students can work together and help each other. Peer conferences can take place either with partners or small groups. During a peer conference the writer reads her work out loud to her partner or group. The listeners respond by asking questions or offering suggestions. If necessary the writer may clarify. She can also ask her listeners questions. The purpose of the peer conference is to help the author see how her work is being understood by readers (listeners) and decide how to improve her writing.

I often use peer conferences at the end of the class. Students meet and share their work with group members. The group members respond and help the writer plan his next steps. If a student doesn't have a finished draft to share, he may read just a portion of what he has written. If he has spent the period developing an idea for writing—perhaps by clustering—he can explain what he has done. It is important that everyone comes to the conference with something to share. Sharing experiences and problems about writing helps to disseminate information and build a feeling of community. Even your most reluctant writers will begin to share through gentle encouragement and cooperation. Peer conferences at the end of class provide a meaningful closure to the day's work.

Before students can be expected to carry out successful peer conferences, they need to know how conferences between students should go. One of the ways you can help them is to sit in on their conferences and model the appropriate behavior. You may listen to a student read his piece and ask a question about it or react to something you liked. (Make suggestions cautiously, since teacher-initiated suggestions can be interpreted as directives.)

The following procedure is also helpful in guiding students in peer conferences. Organize your students into groups of three to five. Group members decide who reads his piece first. This student, the author, reads his piece two times. The first time the listeners merely listen for the overall scope. During the second reading the listeners focus on specific areas. These areas are highlighted on the accompanying "Peer Conference Questions" worksheet. During the early part of the year, you might write separate questions on note cards and assign each listener a different question to answer. This makes it easier. Every time a new author reads, the cards are passed to the person to the left. This ensures that each student will have a chance to listen for a different part of writing. As your students become more familiar with the process, they will be able to listen to more parts and ask their own questions.

Activity 20: Peer Conferences

Explain that the role of students in a peer group is to help other members of the group improve their writing skills. They do this by listening to writers read their papers and then sharing what they like about the papers, as well as suggesting ways to improve them. Since every student in the group gets a chance to read his or her piece, everyone benefits. Because of the experience they gain by helping others improve their work, students become better readers of their own papers. You may choose to distribute copies of "Peer Group Guidelines" and discuss them with your students.

I like to organize peer groups prior to the first day to avoid wasting class time. Not knowing the students, I form the groups randomly, making changes as necessary. In making adjustments I seek balance in each group and try not to leave a shy student with three or four vocal ones who could easily overwhelm him. Likewise, I try to avoid "chatty" combinations.

One of the biggest problems of peer groups is students getting off the subject. In my class, when six groups of four or five students each are in conference at the same time, I cannot oversee every group. To help with management, I appoint a monitor for each group, rotating monitors so that everyone gets a chance. It is the monitor's responsibility to make sure group members stay on the subject of writing. Also, since every group member must have a chance to share, the monitor checks the time and prevents the group from dwelling on any paper too long. I instruct my students to spend between 3 and 5 minutes on each paper. I try not to allow peer conferences to run longer than 20 minutes. More time than that takes away from writing time and also induces students to talk about the latest "news" rather than writing.

I further encourage my students to confer with a partner in an effort to solve writing problems or help in revision. In most cases I permit students to choose their

Peer Conference Questions

Directions: As you listen to the writer's piece, ask yourself the following questions. You may write notes at the bottom of the page.

- What things do I like about this piece?

- What do I want to know more about?

- What is the writer's main point?

- What are some details?

- What suggestions can I offer?

- Is any part of this piece confusing?

- What can be eliminated without losing the author's intention? (words, phrases, sentences, paragraphs)

Notes:

_____

_____

_____

_____

_____

_____

Peer Group Guidelines

The purpose of your peer group is for members to help each other improve their writing. This is done by a writer reading his or her work and having the other group members respond to it. Each member should have a chance to share something, even if it is only a description of an idea for writing. To help your group work successfully, you must follow these rules:

1. Be a good listener. Remain quiet when others are reading and concentrate on their words.

2. Be polite and kind.

3. Remain focused on the writing.

4. Always find something positive in every paper.

5. Always find something that can be improved.

6. Try to offer specific comments, for example,

   • Give what you think was the main idea.

   • Tell what you thought was the best part of the paper and why.

   • Tell the author what details seemed particularly interesting.

   • Tell what you would like to see expanded.

   • Tell the author about any parts you found confusing or redundant.

   • Suggest specific ways to solve problems in the writing, especially any the writer brings up.

own partners, although I quickly separate students who do not work well together. When students realize that you will not tolerate anything except good work during peer conferences, they are more likely to keep on task. Partners work in much the same way as groups. The writer reads her piece and her partner listens and responds to it. The advantage of conference partners is that students need not wait until the entire group meets to confer. Having the freedom to work with a partner also encourages students to cooperate in solving writing problems. While I permit students to confer as necessary, I insist that they do not interfere with anyone else when they are meeting. Providing a separate table or a corner of the room for students to meet reduces the chance of partners disturbing others.

As your students become better writers and more skilled at revision, they will become better at identifying and improving weaknesses in their work. To help them in their efforts, you can distribute copies of the accompanying "Revision Checklist."

As your students become more involved in the writing workshop, they will want to improve their work. They will come to view revision as an important stage of the writing process, seek help with revision, and eventually master the skills for revision that you share with them.

Name _____ Date _____ Class _____

Revision Checklist

_____ 1. Did I write what I wanted to write?

_____ 2. Is my topic focused?

_____ 3. Will my readers understand what I am saying?

_____ 4. Is my writing clear?

_____ 5. Is my opening strong? Does it capture the reader's attention?

_____ 6. Are my main ideas supported with details? Have I used examples?

_____ 7. Does my conclusion contain a final point or summary for my piece?

_____ 8. Is all my information needed? Are there any words, phrases, sentences, or paragraphs that I can cut? Have I cut all clutter?

_____ 9. Are there places I can expand my ideas?

_____ 10. Does my piece show unity? Do all of the parts build to a whole?

_____ 11. Are my paragraphs cohesive and unified? Does each one contain only one main idea?

_____ 12. Is the style right for the subject? Is my style consistent throughout the piece?

_____ 13. What part of this piece do I like the best? Why? _____
_____

_____ 14. What part do I like the least? Why? _____
_____

_____ 15. What part do I feel needs improvement? How can I improve it?
_____

© 1993 by The Center for Applied Research in Education

6

Editing

Editing is the stage of the writing process in which authors evaluate whether they have expressed themselves clearly, using the conventions of standard written English. While major editing should be done after the piece has been revised, editing also occurs during drafting and revision. As she edits, the author concentrates on trimming clutter, tightening the flow, selecting stronger, more vivid words, and correcting any remaining mistakes in mechanics. It is the time to "polish" writing.

When discussing editing with your students, explain that while some editing is natural during drafting and revision as writers pause and reread what they have written, concentrating too much on editing at those times will make it harder for them to write well. Students often become so concerned about mechanics and sentence construction that they constantly stop and search their work for mistakes. Such worry about mechanics draws their attention away from content. It disrupts their thoughts, hinders style, and ruins the flow and rhythm of their words. The time for editing is after the writing is done.

STRATEGIES FOR TEACHING EDITING SKILLS

Before students can edit their work effectively, they must have the skills that are essential for good writing. While the skills taught to sixth graders, for example, will be different from the skills taught to twelfth graders, even young students can learn editing skills within the scope of their curriculum.

When you teach new writing skills, explain them fully, model their use on the blackboard or an overhead projector, and refer to the skill during individual and group conferences. Encourage students to use the skill and monitor that it is being used correctly. Once students understand a skill, they will employ it in their writing and look for it as they edit. The development of editing skills takes time, for they grow out of a student's overall writing experience.

Two resources that authors often rely on during editing are the dictionary and the thesaurus. The understanding of the use of these books is so important that I teach about them early in the school year.

Activity 21: Using a Dictionary

Authors need to know how to use a dictionary. Many students, however, view dictionaries as little more than a place to check spelling. Dictionaries offer much more information than that. If you have enough dictionaries, distribute them so that each student has his or her own. If you don't have enough copies, let students work in groups and share them.

Point out the following features in your dictionaries, and show students examples:

1. The words in a dictionary are listed alphabetically. Guide words that appear at the top of the page make it easy for users to find the word they are looking for.

2. Dictionaries break words into syllables.

3. Dictionaries provide phonetic spellings and syllables to show how words are pronounced.

4. Dictionaries offer the correct spellings of words, their meanings, and parts of speech. Some offer the origin of entry words.

5. Dictionaries show alternate spellings and related forms such as plurals when the form is irregular or hard to spell.

6. Dictionaries offer usage tips; some even show how the word might be used incorrectly.

7. Dictionaries show examples of how a word is used in a sentence.

8. Dictionaries may show synonyms of words.

9. Larger dictionaries may have geographical and biographical sections, maps, and even style books for authors.

Activity 22: Using a Thesaurus

A thesaurus is a book of synonyms and antonyms and is an excellent resource for writers who seek precise words to express their ideas. A thesaurus is not a dictionary, and you should caution your students not to try to use it in that way. If you have copies of thesauruses, distribute them to your students. If you don't have enough copies for everyone in class, allow students to work in groups. Review the thesaurus with them. Point out that words are listed alphabetically with their synonyms and antonyms following. Most thesauruses offer related words, which authors can use if they must continue looking for the word they need. Although thesauruses provide great help to writers, caution your students not to use them to find the longest synonym they can. Some writers mistakenly believe that using "big" words enhances their style. Tell your students that the simplest style is usually the best because it is the clearest. Thesauruses should be used to find the precise words that make writing clear.

You can highlight recently taught skills by maintaining an Editing Skills Bulletin Board. Using poster paper or oak tag (an easel with a roll of paper is also good), set up a bulletin board for editing skills. After teaching a new skill, display it on the board. You can write the skill on a strip of construction paper and tack it to the board. See the example provided.

> Colons (:) are used before a list of items, after the salutation of a business letter, and between the hour and minute in time.

I like to display two or three skills at a time. When I add a new skill, it takes the top position, with the other skills moving down. The bulletin board reminds students of the skills that were recently taught and encourages them to use the skills in their writing and editing. Alternatively, allowing the students to select two or three new skills they may be having trouble with in their writing encourages their involvement in the workshop and heightens interest in editing.

EDITING REMINDERS

Similar to bulletin board checklists are personal editing checklists. I call them "Editing Reminders," an example of which follows. Every week, or every two weeks, depending what best suits your schedule, give each student one or two skills that he or she is to focus on during editing. Here is an example:

> Week(s) of: 11/3 and 11/10
>
> 1. <u>Consistency in tenses.</u>
>
> 2. <u>Watch for spelling of believe, receive, and conceive.</u>
>
> 3. <u>Be sure transitions are smooth.</u>

Explain the purpose and use of the editing reminder sheets. The student retains the editing reminder sheet in her writing folder and refers to it during editing. Each week (or every two weeks) new skills may be added. Successive sheets are paper clipped together so that the student builds a personal packet of skills. I draw the skills from material that has been taught via mini-lessons and conferences. If a skill isn't mastered, I will repeat its use on the reminder sheet or come back to it later in the year. Editing reminder sheets are valuable because they address specific skills that individual students need to work on.

Name _____ Date _____ Class _____

Editing Reminders

Weeks(s) of: _____

_____

_____

_____

_____

Weeks(s) of: _____

_____

_____

_____

_____

Weeks(s) of: _____

_____

_____

_____

_____

EDITING PARTNERS

Peer editing can be done with partners or groups. Before any peer editing takes place, however, instruct your students to reread their revised drafts carefully and edit them individually. Self-editing is an important skill that helps students to become more aware of their writing. Only after self-editing should students take their writing to a partner or peer group for editing.

When working with a partner, the editor reads the author's piece silently, lightly underlining any errors he believes he has found. He may also write comments in the margins or on the bottom of the sheet. I encourage editors to write some things they like about the piece, as well as things they feel need to be improved, because this gives important feedback to the author.

If you provide your editors with the "Editor's Checklist" that follows, they will be guided in their efforts to focus on specific skills. Make the checklists available to students so that they can take the sheets as needed. Without guidance, many students are not sure what to look for while editing. The checklist helps focus their attention on specific skills. In the beginning of the year, it is unlikely that you will have taught all the skills on the list. Since basic skills are listed first, you may instruct your students to ignore the numbers of the skills they haven't learned. Asking editors to sign their work adds formality to the process and encourages students to do a good job. Authors retain the checklists upon completion of editing.

Once the editing is completed, the editor and author go over the piece. If the author disagrees with any of the editor's points, they should first check references and then consult with you. I urge students to check their work themselves because this is when some of the greatest learning occurs.

EDITING GROUPS

Editing groups work much the same way as partners do, but the labor for editing is divided. Groups may contain four to six students. Each member of the group reads the paper, but looks for specific skills. If you are using the "Editor's Checklist," student 1 may edit for the first two skills, student 2 for the next two, and so on.

To ensure that everyone gets a chance to edit for different skills, the responsibility for skills should be rotated. Student 1, for example, who edited for skills 1 and 2 on the first piece, might edit for skills 10 to 12 on the next. Editing groups are good to use at the beginning of the year when students may be unsure of how to edit. To ensure that students are in fact learning editing skills, you should monitor the groups closely, sit in on them, and model the skills.

One of the big problems with editing is that papers get marked up. After a round of editing, the original may be unrecognizable, and the author won't know where to begin making changes. You can avoid this by making photocopies of originals. Editors work with the copies and the author retains the original. Of course this is practical only if you have easy access to a copy machine, but it does simplify the editing process.

If you don't have access to a copier for your workshop, instruct editors to write lightly in pencil. Places where the editor finds an error in punctuation or spelling can

Editor's Checklist

Author _____ Date _____ Class _____

Editor _____

Piece _____

This piece has been edited for the following:

_____ 1. Sentences begin with capital letters.

_____ 2. Sentences have correct ending punctuation.

_____ 3. Sentences are complete.

_____ 4. Paragraphs are indented.

_____ 5. Commas are used in compound sentences, and for the listing of items in a series.

_____ 6. Quotation marks (where necessary) are used correctly.

_____ 7. Apostrophes are used correctly for contractions.

_____ 8. Spelling is correct.

_____ 9. Unnecessary words, phrases, and sentences have been eliminated.

_____ 10. Use of common homonyms (there, their, they're; to, too, two; your, you're) is correct.

_____ 11. Verb tenses are correct.

_____ 12. Subjects and predicates agree.

_____ 13. Pronouns agree with the nouns they replace.

_____ 14. Apostrophes are used correctly for possessive nouns.

_____ 15. Proper nouns and adjectives are capitalized.

_____ 16. Colons are used correctly.

_____ 17. Semi-colons are used correctly.

_____ 18. Underlining (for italics) is used correctly.

_____ 19. Parentheses are used correctly.

_____ 20. Dashes are used correctly.

Editor's Signature _____

be lightly underlined. Every effort should be taken to avoid making the original so hard to read that the author can't decode the editor's comments.

Lightly underlining has another advantage. When students are uncertain of a skill, they may think it's wrong but not be sure. If they stop editing to look the item up, they may lose their focus on the piece. By underlining suspected mistakes, they can complete the editing, discuss the piece with the author, and consult references afterward.

Whenever students work with partners or groups, you must be sure that one student doesn't dominate another. Some student editors with strong personalities can convince a writer he is wrong even when he is not. This is another reason for encouraging students to consult references when disputes over usage, punctuation, grammar, or spelling arise. In cases where there is no definitive answer, the final decision should rest with the writer.

Activity 23: Editor's Marks

To help students with the editing process, distribute copies of the accompanying handout "Editor's Marks." The symbols make minor corrections easy. In discussing the editor's marks, explain that professional editors and authors use the symbols with their work. The symbols may be used during revision and self-editing, too. Suggest that students keep the sheet in their writing folders and refer to it during revision and editing. You might also display a large copy.

After students have completed editing and have made any needed corrections, but before they do their final copies, have them put their papers in the editing box. Do not edit pieces during class, because there are too many other demands and your time will probably be better spent working with students on the development of their pieces. As soon as students put their pieces in the box, they begin new work.

Read the edited papers quickly for content and then once again more slowly for mechanics, noting any weaknesses and errors. Encourage students by writing notes of praise when they have done well.

During class, confer with students individually about their papers. Try to address one or two mistakes that they make often. Confronting students with an assortment of mistakes will only overwhelm them; they won't know where to begin to correct all the errors. Rather than teaching them how to improve weak skills, you might be teaching them to hate writing.

Although you show students their mistakes, and they make corrections, many students make the same mistakes again. That is common. It may take a few pieces for them to master a skill, but they will. Learning often occurs in small steps.

PROOFREADING

Proofreading should be done after the piece has been revised and edited and is in its final form. The purpose of proofreading is to find any remaining errors in mechanics that may have slipped through revision. Because it is the last step of the writing process before publishing, proofreading is vital. You must demand that published pieces contain as few mistakes as possible. Publishing is the showcase of writing, and excellence should be the goal.

Editor's Marks

Symbol	Meaning	Example
¶	new paragraph	for vacation.¶Soon . . .
≡	capitalize	North a̱merica
/	lower case	The P̸olitician shook hands.
↶ ○	move	They went after skating (home)
∧	insert a letter	high scho͡l
∧	insert a word	They ∧ late for the game. *were*
⌃	insert a comma	pencils⌄ pens, and paper.
⊙	add a period	He arrived at work⊙
ℓ	delete a letter	Are you the̸re?
ℓ	delete a word	He went the the wrong way.
∽	switch letters	The game w̶s̶a̶ exciting.
∽	switch words	They saw all it of.
⌄" ⌄"	quotation marks	⌄"Goodby," she said.
Ⓝⓒ	not clear	Ⓝⓒ Tomorrow was the race.
#	separate	They drove to⌗the shore.
‿	combine	The earth‿quake was awful.

Proofreading is difficult. I tell my students to read slowly during proofing and concentrate on mechanics. I suggest that they read each sentence to see if it stands alone. Are all the words spelled and used correctly? Are proper nouns and adjectives capitalized? Is the ending punctuation correct? Do subjects and verbs agree? Are pronouns used correctly? Any mistakes should be underlined lightly with pencil and corrected after the proofreading is completed.

Many people view editing as a time merely for catching and correcting mistakes in writing. It can be much more. When students self-edit, they have the chance to put themselves in the shoes of their readers and see if what they have written is what they intended.

7

Publishing

Publishing (sometimes called "postwriting") is crucial to your writing workshop. Students need to share their writing with others; they need others to read and react to their words. Your students will write better if they know their writing will be shared.

Publishing in the writing workshop refers to the many ways students may share their writing, from magazines to peer groups to the author's chair. Because of its importance, publishing should be a regular event in your classroom.

THE AUTHOR'S CHAIR

One of the simplest ways to share writing is through "the author's chair." A student takes center stage (a chair at the front of the classroom, for instance) and reads his or her work to the class. The other students become the audience and may ask questions or offer comments. The feedback is immediate.

Some teachers like to reserve the author's chair for the end of each week; others allow students to read their work as they finish. I like to have the author's chair two or three times a week. On the days we do the author's chair, I usually have two or three students read their pieces. If students don't volunteer, I will ask individuals to read their work. I try to get everyone involved during the year, but I will not force anyone. Sometimes I will read the work of a shy student, with that student's permission, of course. As they see more and more of their friends share writing via the author's chair, most students eventually volunteer.

Similar to the author's chair is "author's day." You might set aside one day each week, or a day or two each month, to honor your student authors. On author's day, students may go to other classes to give readings of their work, or you might set up a special display or bulletin board to show the work of student authors. Including photographs of your students with their work can make an impressive exhibit.

PEER GROUP SHARING

On the days I do not have the author's chair scheduled, students meet in peer groups at the end of class and share their work. I reserve about 10 minutes for this. To keep the groups moving I appoint monitors; students watch the time and make sure that no one dominates the meeting and that everyone shares. As I circulate, I try to sit in on each group and model appropriate behavior. If I am unable to be a part of each group on any day, I'll make a mental note to start next time with the groups I missed.

All students are encouraged to share their work. They may read their piece, or a part of it, or they may simply tell others what they have been working on. The group members may comment, ask questions, or offer suggestions. I like to have my students share each day with the class, with a peer group, or with a peer partner because of the feedback they receive. Moreover, when they share each day, the feeling of community and the desire to share grow.

CLASS MAGAZINES

Class magazines are another way of sharing the writing of your students. Class magazines may be simple—stapled collections of students' work written in long-hand—or more elaborate efforts that are typed and illustrated. I publish at least one short magazine each month, with a longer one at least twice a year. Publishing magazines may sound like a lot of work, but it's not as much as you may think.

Following are the typical materials and equipment needed to produce a magazine for your writing workshop:

Materials

Writing paper, typewriter or computer paper, graph paper, ditto masters (if you will be using a duplicator to produce your magazine)
Black pens, erasable pens, pencils, markers, White out, white tape, scissors, lettering stencils, transfer letters, glue, paste, stapler, rulers

Equipment

Typewriters or word processors, photocopier or duplicator

A class magazine may be a simple collection of student writings. If you have copies of magazines from previous classes, pass them around so that students see what a class magazine is like. It is possible that many of them have never been involved in the production of a class magazine.

Be sure to discuss requirements both for material and format. Will the magazine contain only fiction, only nonfiction, or both? Will it include poetry? Will any types of stories be unacceptable? If you are accepting handwritten work, it must be neat and written in black ink with no cross outs. Also be sure to tell them when the deadline is. The deadline should be a firm one and allow you enough time to organize the compiled material. Finally, emphasize that work must be high quality—every attempt must be made to publish material with sound ideas and correct mechanics.

A week or two before the magazine is scheduled to be printed, ask students to submit stories, articles, and poems for the magazine. You may brainstorm magazine names with your students, or you may call it, for example, *The Collected Stories of Mrs. Smith's Writing Classes, Volume I.* If you include the date, at the end of the year, students who save the magazines will have several issues, which when put in order will detail the class's writing experience.

Whenever I publish a magazine, I produce enough copies for every student in the class and several extras for the principal, for exhibits in the school media center, and for hallway displays. It is important for students to know that you think their work is worthy to share with people outside the classroom.

In addition to the monthly magazine, you can publish special collections. After a mini-lesson on limericks, for example, several students wrote limericks, and I published them in a magazine.

If you team teach or are departmentalized, you may decide to publish magazines for each class or include the work of students from all classes in a grade-level magazine. In either case, you should begin collecting work for your magazine in advance. If a student writes what you feel is an excellent piece, ask her if she would like it to be published. Even if the magazine isn't scheduled to be printed for another three weeks, I will put the piece in a separate folder. If it needs any final revisions, have the student do them now rather than later. Once the piece is done, it will stay in the folder until the magazine is ready for printing. By collecting work early, you reduce the problems of trying to gather material for the magazine the day before printing.

My magazines are produced on a photocopier and are bound with staples. They can just as easily be done on a duplicator, in which case, final copies would be written on ditto masters or made into ditto masters. The simplest magazines are collections of students' writing done in longhand. I demand neat handwriting or clear printing in black ink. Erasable pens are helpful because they eliminate the need for White out on final copies.

It is impractical to attempt to have every magazine typed, unless students can do most of the typing themselves (preferably on a computer, which allows for easy proofreading). If your students cannot help with typing, try building a network of parent volunteers to reduce the load. You can send a letter home, explaining that you plan to produce magazines containing the writings of your students and that you need help with the typing. Some years I get more parents than others, but every year I get enough to help. If you have access to word processors in your school, and your students are proficient at keyboards, they can enter stories. If you have desktop publishing software, which is available for many computers, you can turn out exceptional magazines. I also encourage students to do their own magazines that I produce on the photocopier. Two of my students created a monthly magazine they titled *Video Game Review.* Each month they summarized several popular video games and offered tips on how their readers could be successful playing the games. I'm sure that they enjoyed doing their research. The magazine ran three to four pages, which they produced on their own computers in a fine effort month after month.

Tips for Producing Class Magazines

Producing a class magazine is not as hard as it may seem. Remembering the following points makes it even easier.

- Start collecting material early. Have students revise pieces ahead of time and store them in folders. If you are doing magazines for more than one class, keep separate folders of pieces for each class.
- Set standards of what is acceptable. Will you accept stories, articles, and poems? Or will the magazine contain only fiction, only nonfiction, or only poems? What types of material will be unacceptable (for example, gory horror stories)? Also emphasize that all work must be original and be careful that students do not plagiarize.
- Organize the magazine in parts. Do pages one through four, then five through eight, and so on. This breaks down the job of producing the magazine to manageable parts.
- If you intend to type the magazine, enlist the help of parent volunteers. If students have access to word processors, they might be able to help. Desktop publishing software can be used to produce outstanding magazines.
- If you intend to include artwork, ask your students to do line drawings that illustrate the writing. Caution them that elaborate drawings with much detail may not reproduce well. Cut the drawings out and use white tape or paste to position them on the page. Permitting students to draw directly on written pages risks mistakes that might require that the page be redone.
- For titles, use transfer letters or stencils. Light, blue-line graph paper is useful for positioning letters as the blue lines will not reproduce on photocopiers.
- If possible, reproduce the magazine on both sides of each page. This will improve the appearance. Magazines can be reproduced either on photocopiers or duplicators. If using a duplicator, however, you will need to create ditto masters.
- Before printing, appoint student proofreaders to catch last-minute errors.
- Print enough copies of your magazine for students, as well as your principal, and for displays throughout your school.

© 1993 by The Center for Applied Research in Education

Along with simple magazines, I publish two or three major ones each year. To generate enthusiasm, you can brainstorm possible titles with your class. This way, the class takes ownership of the magazine. Feeling that it is "theirs" will motivate them to work harder for it. I encourage students to submit stories, articles, poems, and puzzles, and I collect their work well in advance. When students see their classmates writing different pieces, they are more willing to try new forms.

The major magazines include artwork. Students do line drawings that tie in with the writing. For example, a science fiction story might be illustrated with aliens, spaceships, or exotic backgrounds. The artist reads the story and creates illustrations that he or she feels highlight the action. If you have students illustrate your magazines, caution them not to use too much shading, which won't reproduce well on photocopiers or ditto masters.

While most teachers produce magazines on photocopiers and duplicators, there is another option. If your high school has a print shop, you might be able to have your class's magazines printed there. The relationship you develop with the print shop teacher will be a reciprocal one. Your students receive quality magazines and the print shop students work on a meaningful project.

USING A WORD PROCESSOR OR TYPEWRITER

Word processors and typewriters are excellent aids to the writing workshop. Students who have access to these machines can turn out high-quality material. Unfortunately, just because you have access to this equipment doesn't mean that students will be able to utilize it easily.

The best way to implement the use of word processors or typewriters is through an introductory activity. Explain to your students that they will be able to use the machines for their writing.

Divide your class into groups of 5 to 10 students and introduce them to the equipment. You might need to repeat this activity during a few class periods so that everyone gets an introduction to the machines.

For typewriters you will need to show the students the functioning of special code keys or commands. You should also show them how to set margins, mark tabs, and put paper in.

For word processors briefly explain how the equipment works and demonstrate by using a sample paragraph that you enter and print. Show students how they can delete, add, and move text; save their pieces; format; and print. It will take students some time to master the word processing system, but not as long as you might expect.

Once students realize how much easier it is to store and edit their pieces on the word processor, they will want to do all their writing there. Unless you have enough equipment for every student, you will need to use a sign-up sheet to ensure that everyone gets a chance. I limit students to two class periods per piece.

Advising your students that they should do their prewriting before they come to the word processor so that they are ready to enter their drafts ensures that time at the word processor is well spent. After a student enters his draft, he should print it and do revisions in pencil on the copy. While he does this, another student may use the word processor to enter her piece. In this way the equipment is utilized efficiently.

During revision I confer with students, and afterward they revise their pieces on the word processor. Upon completion of revision the final copy is printed.

Whether using typewriters or word processors, it is helpful to display copies of the basic commands on file cards and tape them by each machine. I also include basic typing formats: two spaces after end punctuation and colons, one after commas and semicolons. I prefer students to double-space their pieces and single-space letters with an extra space between paragraphs. Writing these directions on file cards eliminates the need for students constantly to ask you. You might also display basic commands and typing instructions on wall posters.

PRODUCING BOOKS WRITTEN BY STUDENTS

While much of the writing of your students will be published as individual pieces in magazines, featured in displays, and shared through peer groups, you may also publish books written by your students. Student books may be relatively short—a book of poems, for example—or a long work that runs a hundred pages or more.

Some high school print shops can provide perfect binding (glued binding) as well as laminated or multicolored covers. You might be able to develop a cross-curriculum relationship with the print shop teacher.

Some elementary and middle school art teachers can help you produce books written by your students. In fact, working with the art teacher to produce books in art class that your students wrote in your writing workshop can be a fine interdisciplinary project.

You can also produce a book in your classroom. The simplest way is to use a photocopier for printing and staples for the binding. A heavier weight paper, thin cardboard, or report covers will make durable book covers. If you are producing only one copy per student, you may allow students to create a cover with an explosion of color. Some computers have graphics software that can be used to make attractive covers.

If you wish to make more elaborate books, there are several sources that describe in detail the necessary steps. *How to Make Your Own Books* by Harvey Weiss (New York: Thomas Y. Crowell Company, 1974) offers several options for bookmaking that can be done in the classroom. *Creative Bookbinding* by Pauline Johnson (Seattle and London: University of Washington Press, 1973) explains the making of several types of books, including accordion books, booklets, and signature books. There are undoubtedly many more good sources in your local library. Check under "Bookbinding" or "Bookmaking" in the card catalog.

STILL MORE WAYS TO SHARE

Along with class magazines and books, there are many other ways to share the writing of your students. One of the easiest is to photocopy individual pieces and distribute copies to the class. If your school relies on a duplicator, have your students write their final copies on ditto masters.

District or PTA magazines and newsletters are another option for sharing. You will find most of these receptive to good material submitted by students.

Local newspapers are yet another possible source for publishing. If the paper doesn't normally carry the work of students, call the editor and ask if the paper would be willing to run a column about your school, written by your students.

Writing contests are another possibility. Be alert for information about contests your students might be able to enter. In our school the local police department runs a drug awareness program. Part of the program is a poetry contest about the harmful effects of drugs. You might also sponsor your own writing contest within your school or, if you are part of a large district, among schools. Teachers from various grade levels whose students are not participating may serve as judges.

In your sharing of the writing of your students don't neglect the use of bulletin boards, hallway displays, and library exhibits. These are easy ways to make the work of your students available to others.

Another way of sharing is for students to give readings of their work. You might arrange for your students to visit another class and read their work to the students there. On another day those students may visit your class and read their work to your class. A twist on this activity is to have older students read their work to younger ones.

Finally, you shouldn't hesitate to share your own writing with students. When a teacher shares his or her writing, students see a wonderful example of an adult using a skill they are learning. It adds to the importance of writing.

SUBMITTING TO MAGAZINES

One of the most exciting things that can happen to students of your writing workshop is to have their work accepted for publication by a magazine. The odds are stiff, but the reward of acceptance justifies the hard work.

Mention submitting their writing to a magazine and students will rush for envelopes. Of course, this is the quickest way to rejection.

Students will increase their chances for acceptance of their pieces by studying several past issues of the magazines they are considering. (It is helpful if you obtain some copies for them, perhaps from your school or local library. Students might also write for sample copies from publishers. Some publishers provide free copies; others charge a nominal fee.) Studying past issues will help students to see what kind of material each magazine prefers and to avoid writing about a topic that has been handled in a recent issue. When students are studying the magazine, they should look not only at topics but also at how the material is developed. What kind of leads do the articles have? How are the stories written? What is the tone, the style? Attention to such details can result in acceptances.

You should also discuss rejection. Point out that many pieces are rejected because of the strong competition. Receiving a rejection does not always mean that the writing of a student is poor. It may be that the editor at the magazine has a similar piece in stock or that the piece is not right for the magazine. Emphasize that all authors suffer rejection.

Some publications prefer query letters to manuscripts. Students should write to the editors of these magazines first, describing their proposed article to see if the editor is interested. They should enclose a SASE (self- addressed, stamped envelope) for a reply. Encourage students to submit to only one magazine at a time, unless editorial guidelines state that the magazine will consider multiple submissions.

An effective query letter is concise. It should explain the proposed article and why the magazine's readers would enjoy it. If the student has any qualifications for writing the piece, he or she should include them.

Activity 24: Submitting Student Writing to Magazines

Explain to your students that submitting their work (which will now be called manuscripts) to magazines that publish the writing of students is one of the best ways of sharing, because the author can reach thousands of readers. Tell them that because the competition is heavy, they should submit only their best work.

You might wish to distribute copies of the accompanying "Tips for Submitting to Magazines." Discussing the sheet will highlight the steps your students should take for sending their work to editors.

Activity 25: Writing a Query Letter

Distribute copies of the accompanying "Sample Query Letter." Discuss what a query letter is and go over its parts. Note that the first two paragraphs explain the background of the proposed article, the third asks the editor if she is interested in seeing the article, and the fourth states the author's qualifications. The letter ends with a thank you.

*MARKETS THAT PUBLISH THE WRITING OF STUDENTS*_____

There are many markets that publish the writing of students. However, they are not well publicized, and many teachers and students are unaware of them.

Since markets change, the needs of editors vary, and magazines may merge or fold, I suggest you contact or check a current issue of the markets below before having your students send material to them. A helpful resource is the *Market Guide for Young Writers* by Kathy Henderson. Your library might have a copy, but the guide is also available through Betterway Publications, Inc., Box 219, Crozet, VA 22932. The cost at the time of this printing was $12.95. It offers detailed information about more than 100 markets and contests that seek manuscripts from students. *Writer's Market*, edited by Mark Kissling and published by F & W Publications, 1507 Dana Avenue, Cincinnati, OH 45207, provides detailed market listings for beginning and professional authors. Older students might find it helpful. The cost at the time of this printing was $26.95; however, many libraries carry copies.

Several magazines have provided a steady showcase for the writing of students. These are listed in the accompanying "Markets for Student Writers."

The writing workshop provides the environment for students to write the way real authors do. It allows for prewriting, drafting, revising, editing, and publishing. With students working individually or with a partner or in a small group, the writing workshop is a classroom of activity and diversity. It is a place of self-discovery, learning, and growth.

Tips for Submitting to Magazines

Following these suggestions can increase your chances of having an article, story, or poem accepted for publication by a magazine:

- Become familiar with the magazine you intend to submit to. Study several past issues to gain an understanding of the material the editors use, recent topics, and the tone and style of the magazine. Don't do a topic that has already been done. Strive for freshness.
- When a magazine asks for queries only, don't send the manuscript.
- When submitting to a magazine, always include a SASE (self-addressed, stamped envelope).
- Unless editors at a magazine will consider simultaneous submissions (the sending of a query or manuscript to several magazines at the same time), send to only one at a time.
- Always follow the magazine's guidelines. If the editors want articles or stories of 1,000 words, don't send pieces of 500 or 1,500.
- If you send a photocopy, be sure it is clear and has crisp lettering.
- Your material should be typed on standard 8½" by 11" white bond paper. Avoid erasable paper, which smudges easily. Keep margins of at least 1" on every side. Your name and address should appear at the top left corner of the title page with the word count, rounded to the nearest hundred, at the top right. The title with the author's name should be centered on the first page, about one-third of the way down. Starting with page two, your last name and a few key words of the title should appear at the top left of every page. This is called the pageheading and makes it easier for editors to find pages of your manuscript should they become separated. Numbers of the pages may be at the top right or centered. Use paper clips, not staples, to keep the manuscript together.
- Always keep a copy of everything you mail. You won't be the first author to have a manuscript get lost.
- Include a short cover letter when you send your work to a magazine. Avoid trying to tell the editor everything about your manuscript in the cover letter; let your work speak for itself.
- Set up a chart recording when and where you sent your manuscript. If it is rejected, cross off that magazine and send the manuscript to another. A rejection doesn't mean your piece is no good. It may be simply that the magazine couldn't use it.

Sample Query Letter

© 1993 by The Center for Applied Research in Education

Author's Name
Address
City, State, ZIP Code
Date

Editor's Name
Name of Magazine
Address
City, State, ZIP Code

Dear (Editor's Name or Dear Sir or Madam):

Pollution is a serious problem for everyone. While many adults belong to groups that fight pollution, kids can get involved, too.

At Jefferson Middle School, students have organized Young People Against Pollution. It is a club that seeks to make young people aware of the problems caused by pollution. We also organize activities that help fight pollution. This year we cleared litter from our town's parks, and wrote letters to the state assembly about reducing air pollution. We plan more activities in the coming year.

Would (Magazine's Name) be interested in an article about how eighth graders can fight pollution? In the article I would tell your readers about our club and explain how they may organize a similar one.

I feel confident I can write this article. I am a founder of Young People Against Pollution and serve as its current president.

Thank you for your time.

Sincerely,

(Author's Name)

Markets for Student Writers

Because of the constant changes that occur in publishing, contact the following markets before sending material to them.

- *Child Life*, 1100 Waterway Boulevard, Box 567, Indianapolis, IN 46206. Stories, poems, jokes, riddles. Ages 9-11.
- *Children's Digest*, 1100 Waterway Boulevard, Box 567, Indianapolis, IN 46206. Stories, poems, jokes, riddles. Preteens.
- *Creative with Words Publications*, Box 223226, Carmel, CA 93922-3226. Poetry and prose on varying themes. Write for details.
- *Cricket*, 315 5th Street, Box 300, Peru, IL 61354. Contests. Rules in each issue. Ages 6-12.
- *Crusader Magazine*, Box 7259, Grand Rapids, MI 49510. Articles with a Christian perspective. Boys, ages 9-14.
- *Highlights for Children*, 803 Church Street, Honesdale, PA 18431. Letters, jokes, riddles, short prose, poetry. Ages up to 12.
- *Jack and Jill*, 1100 Waterway Boulevard, Box 567, Indianapolis, IN 46206. Stories, poems, jokes, riddles. Ages 7-10.
- *Merlyn's Pen, The National Magazine of Student Writing*, Box 1058, East Greenwich, RI 02818. Stories, poems, essays, reviews. Ages 11-15.
- *Poetry, USA*, Fort Mason Center, Building D, San Francisco, CA 94123. Poetry.
- *Quarterly Magazine*, Children's Express, 30 Cooper Square, New York, NY 10003. Stories, articles, poetry. Write for details.
- *Read*, 245 Long Hill Road, Middletown, CT 06457. Short poems and stories.
- *Scholastic Writing Contests*, 730 Broadway, New York, NY 10003. Write for details. Ages 11-18.
- *Seventeen*, 850 Third Avenue, New York, NY 10022. Short fiction, poetry. Annual fiction contest. Girls, ages 13-19.
- *Skipping Stones*, Box 3939, Eugene, OR 97403. Stories, poems, book and movie reviews.
- *TQ (TeenQuest)*, Box 82808, Lincoln, NE 68501. Book reviews, first-person articles, poetry. Teens.
- *Writing!*, c/o Student Writing Department, 60 Revere Drive, Northbrook, IL 60062-1563. Fiction, nonfiction, poetry. Grades 7-12.

Part Two

USING MINI-LESSONS IN THE WRITING WORKSHOP

Mini-lessons are a fine way to begin your writing workshops. They provide a time when the entire class is drawn together and you may address everyone at once. Mini-lessons afford you the opportunity to introduce students to various types of writing, discuss specific writing techniques, teach basic language skills, and share information about writing.

Mini-lessons should be short, not more than 5 to 10 minutes, and should focus on one topic. Your students may use the information they learn in mini-lessons right away or may not incorporate it into their writing for some time. Reviewing the information of your mini-lessons during individual and small-group conferences will provide your students with the reinforcement needed to master fully the more difficult skills.

The mini-lessons that follow are divided into three kinds:

1. Mini-lessons for Types of Writing

2. Mini-lessons for the Art of Writing

3. Mini-lessons for the Mechanics of Writing

All are arranged in a lesson plan format. Background information is provided, followed by specific procedures, and, where necessary, reproducibles. Some mini-lessons also include extensions, which in most cases are activities that you may wish to use depending upon your class and schedule. While they are not essential to the actual mini-lesson, they provide additional practice on the topic of the lesson.

Together with the activities that appear in Part I, the mini-lessons of Part II offer a wide assortment of topics and skills you can present to your students. However, it is also likely that you will develop others, based upon the particular needs of your class. Feel free to use the provided mini-lessons as models to create your own mini-lessons.

Mini-lessons for Types of Writing

MINI-LESSON 1:
WRITING PERSONAL NARRATIVES

Narratives are compositions in which the writer tells about a personal experience—they are brief accounts of something that happened to the writer. A focused main idea, strong details, and examples are the keys to effective narratives. Personal narratives provide good opportunities for students to write because the students draw upon their own experiences. You will find that much of the writing that goes on in your writing workshop will be personal narrative.

Procedure:

1. Discuss the features of a narrative with your students.
2. Read a narrative to the class. This may be a narrative written by a former student (be sure to get permission) or a narrative of your own. If you wish, distribute copies of (or project) the accompanying "The Big Splash." Either read it aloud to your students or ask your students to read it silently. If you read it, be sure to read with feeling.
3. Emphasize the features of the narrative you chose to read by pointing out specific examples.
4. Note that narratives are usually told in the first person (using "I").
5. Mention that while most narratives are told in chronological order, some use flashback (see Mini-lesson 37) or rearrange time order to tell the narrative in a more interesting way.

A Big Splash

I remember not being able to sleep. By four I was up and dressed and bounding into my uncle Bob's room. That's how you are when you're ten years old and going fishing with your favorite uncle who just came back from the navy.

I had to wake him up. But by six-thirty we were at the dock on the lake.

Uncle Bob instructed me to get into the boat so that he could hand me the fishing gear. There was plenty of it—poles, tackle boxes, bait box, the cooler that contained our lunches, a long-handled net, and extra sweatshirts. I climbed into the boat thinking, "This is gonna be great."

He handed me my small tackle box and pole first. I put them on the back seat of the row boat and promptly opened the box and began looking for just the right hook. After all, there was no time to waste. The biggest bass in the state was waiting for me!

So involved was I that I didn't notice my uncle piling the rest of our gear into the boat. He had one foot on the dock and one on the boat. I also didn't notice that as I fuddled about in back, the boat began to ease away from the dock.

"Pull the boat in with the line," said my uncle. I turned. I wasn't sure what he meant. I did see him with one foot on the dock and one on the boat. They were spread precariously far apart.

"Pull the boat in!" he said more urgently.

Realizing what was happening, I jumped up to get to the front of the boat. But my movement caused the boat to slip farther from the dock.

"Pull—"

It was too late. My uncle Bob made a big splash.

MINI-LESSON 2:
WRITING ESSAYS

An essay is a short piece in which a writer discusses a specific topic. Since your students will often be required to write essays in school to answer test questions, out of school for competency tests, or in application to college, the essay is an important form of writing for students to learn.

Procedure:

1. Discuss the essay form with your students.

2. Explain that the typical essay follows the format of introduction, body, and conclusion. The author states the purpose or main point of the essay in the introduction, explains the main idea in the body, and concludes with a final point that adds more weight to his arguments.

3. Emphasize that essays should be written in a clear concise style. All main ideas must be supported with details or examples.

4. Distribute copies of (or project), and read the accompanying sample essay, "Slowing Global Warming by Saving Energy." Point out the introduction, body, and conclusion.

Extension:

- Suggest to your students that they read other examples of essays, which can be found on the op-ed pages of many newspapers and in many magazines.

Slowing Global Warming by Saving Energy

One of the easiest ways to slow global warming is to save energy. The burning of fossil fuels, for instance, releases carbon dioxide into the atmosphere. The carbon dioxide traps the sun's heat and is one of the causes of global warming. By reducing the amount of fossil fuels we use, we will reduce the amount of carbon dioxide in the atmosphere, and global warming will slow.

There are many ways we can reduce the amount of fossil fuels that we burn. Since most homes are heated by burning natural gas or oil, keeping the thermostats a few degrees lower in the winter can save much energy.

The electricity that most homes use is produced by burning coal, oil, or natural gas. The less electricity we use, the less fossil fuel power plants need. Even something as simple as shutting off the light in an empty room can lead to big energy savings if it is done in homes across the country.

Reducing the amount of gasoline we use is another way to save. Gasoline is refined from oil. When it is burned, carbon dioxide is given off. We can reduce the amount of gasoline we use by car pooling and taking mass transit.

Reducing the amount of energy each of us uses can conserve the fossil fuels we use. Each of us will then be helping to slow global warming.

MINI-LESSON 3:
STRATEGIES FOR ANSWERING ESSAY TEST QUESTIONS

To answer essay test questions effectively, students must know the subject matter and write clearly. Just knowing the facts isn't good enough; they must be able to analyze, organize, and explain those facts. This is often a challenge because time is at a premium.

Procedure:

1. Explain that the first step in answering an essay question is to understand precisely what the question is asking. Tell your students to look for key words, which can help them determine the focus of the essay. Common key words may ask essay writers to *identify, compare, contrast, discuss, explain, analyze,* or *summarize* information about a topic. Make sure that your students know what these key words mean.

2. Write the following steps to answering essay questions on the board or an overhead projector and briefly discuss them with your students:

   a. Read the question carefully. Look for key words and decide exactly what the question is asking.

   b. Study the question to get clues for organizing.

   c. Use scrap paper to write your introduction. It should state your main point, because this will help you to organize your information.

   d. List major ideas and some notes that you will include in your essay.

   e. If you have time, rewrite the essay or at least check for errors.

3. Mention that since time is usually a factor during essay tests, students should write as well as they can the first time.

MINI-LESSON 4:
WRITING HOW-TO ARTICLES

How-to articles are a popular form of nonfiction writing. The how-to article explains how something can be done. Countless examples of how-to books and articles can be found in libraries and bookstores.

Since how-tos can be written about special talents or skills, they are a form of writing that most students can easily attempt. I remember one student who usually had little interest in writing. He did, however, like to fish. He enjoyed the sport so much that he made his own fishing lures. After explaining how-to articles via a mini-lesson, I suggested to him that he might write a piece about how his classmates could design and make their own fishing lures. The piece turned out to be the best he wrote that year.

Procedure:

1. Explain what a how-to article is.

2. Distribute copies of (or project) the accompanying sample how-to article, "How to Make a Budget." Read the article aloud or have students read it silently.

3. Emphasize that since a how-to tells the reader how to do something, the writing must be clear and logical. The writer must be sure that she doesn't leave any steps out or readers will become lost.

4. Suggest that before writing a how-to, students list their ideas and put them in step-by-step order. Writing down their information will enable them to see if an important step or detail is missing.

Extension:

• Ask your students to review magazines they receive at home or magazines that are available in your school or local library and identify examples of how-to articles. If possible, students should bring the magazines to class and share them with peer groups.

How to Make a Budget

Have you ever run out of money at the end of the month? If you have, you're like countless other people. And, like many of them, you can avoid this problem by making a budget.

To make a budget, you need to balance your income and expenses. First, you must list all of your expenses. Include everything that you regularly spend money on. For example, you should list the money you need for clothes, lunch, going out with your friends, or entertainment (like tapes or CDs). If you intend to save some money each month by putting it in the bank, count this as an expense too. It's important not to leave anything out. After listing your expenses, add them up.

Next, list your sources of income. This includes any allowance, as well as money you earn doing chores or working.

Now subtract your expenses from your income. Money left over is called a surplus. You may spend it, or choose to save it. If you do not have enough money to cover your expenses, you must either increase your income or reduce your expenses.

Although most people will agree that sticking to a budget can be harder than making one, they will also agree that a good budget is an excellent tool for keeping track of your money.

MINI-LESSON 5:
WRITING STRAIGHT NEWS ARTICLES

Straight news articles are written in clear, concise sentences. They focus on facts and develop their material around the five W's and how: *What* happened? *When* did it happen? *Where* did it happen? *Who* was involved? *Why* did it happen? And *how* did it happen? Most, if not all, of these questions are usually answered in the lead (first paragraph) in straight news. The rest of the article offers details, organized so that the most important information comes first. This structure, an inverted pyramid organization, enables busy readers to gain the essential information quickly and allows editors to drop the final paragraphs if they run out of space.

Procedure:

1. Explain that the typical newspaper article is developed around answering the five W's and how.

2. Explain the importance of the lead.

3. Distribute copies of (or project) the accompanying sample newspaper article, "Bat Attacks Alarm Town." Read it with your class and explain how it answers the questions

   What? Bats attack people.

   When? At dusk, this past week.

   Where? In town.

   Who? Townspeople.

   Why? The reason is being investigated.

   How? Flying around people's heads and faces.

Extensions:

• Ask students to bring in newspapers from home. Point out that the typical newspaper contains several sections: the main news, features — which do not follow the structure of main news articles — editorial page, finance, TV and movie listings, the weather, sports, fashion, the obituaries, comics, and classified ads. Discuss the sections, particularly the editorials and features.

• Ask students to bring in newspapers from home. Divide students into groups of four to six and ask them to review different articles and identify how they are structured. Each student should take at least one article and look for the five W's and how. To help them, hand out copies of "Taking Apart a Newspaper Article." After reviewing their articles, students should share their findings with their groups, summarizing the article and explaining how the articles answer the five W's and how.

• Organize a class newspaper to give students experience in newspaper writing.

• With another teacher, "stage" an event in the classroom and ask students to report on it in a straight news story. Discuss the variety of approaches that result.

Bat Attacks Alarm Town

Darden's Mill, April 17

At a public meeting last night, residents of Darden's Mill voiced alarm over a recent flurry of "bat attacks" in their neighborhood. Mayor Paul Burke directed Police Chief Steve Harkins to contact experts on bats at the State University for help in dealing with the bats' strange behavior.

The first reported attack was April 12. Just after dusk a bat attacked Robert Williams as he was taking out his garbage. "The bat kept circling around my head, like a big mosquito buzzing in my ear," Williams said. Although shaken by the attack, Williams was unhurt.

At least four more attacks have occurred in the same area since then. Each attack came around dusk, and in each case the bats repeatedly flew around the head and face of their targets. So far, no injuries have been reported.

That is little consolation to frightened townspeople. "Those bats might be rabid," said Audrey Martin, who was attacked at her home last night. She worries about her two small children.

Although bats have been known to carry rabies, this doesn't seem to be the case here. "No one has been bitten, and there is no evidence that these bats are diseased," said Chief Harkins.

The mayor concurs. "There's no need to panic until we find out why the bats are behaving like this," he said. He asks people to remain cautious but calm until the researchers from the university complete their investigation.

Name _____ Date _____ Class _____

Taking Apart a Newspaper Article

Directions: Select a news article. Read it carefully, and identify how it answers the questions: What? Who? When? Where? Why? How? Share your findings with your group.

What? _____

_____

_____

Who? _____

_____

_____

When? _____

_____

_____

Where? _____

_____

_____

Why? _____

_____

_____

How? _____

_____

_____

MINI-LESSON 6:
PERSUASIVE WRITING_____

Persuasive writings, often called opinion pieces or personal essays, express an author's opinion about a topic. Many newspapers contain op-ed pages or sections of "Letters to the Editor" where the newspapers' readers can publish their opinions about problems or controversial subjects. Some magazines also carry opinion pieces. The authors of these pieces often try to persuade readers to adopt a particular view on an issue.

Procedure:

1. Explain what persuasive writing is.

2. Distribute copies of (or project) the accompanying "Save Trees and the Environment by Recycling Newspapers." Read it with your students.

3. Explain that all persuasive writing pieces follow the structure of introduction, body, and conclusion. Point out the three parts on the sample.

   a. Note that the *introduction* contains a strong opening sentence that hooks the reader. It also mentions the problem.

   b. Point out that the author develops her position in the *body*. In the typical persuasive piece, authors use facts, examples, and explanations to support main ideas. Depending on the complexity of the topic, the body may be one or several paragraphs long.

   c. Explain that in the *conclusion* the author offers suggestions of what should be done about the problem. Often the author will call on readers to become involved or take personal action. A strong ending sentence emphasizes the main point of the piece.

Extension:

- Distribute copies of "Analyzing a Persuasive Essay." Instruct your students to find examples of persuasive essays in newspapers and magazines, and then analyze them by completing the worksheet. Students should share the essays and their analyses with their peer groups.

Analyzing a Persuasive Essay

Directions: Select a persuasive essay and analyze it. Answer the following questions and share the essay and your findings with your group.

1. Title of essay: _____

Publication in which it appeared: _____

_____

Volume (if magazine): _____ Date: _____

2. What is the author's hook? _____

_____

3. What is the main idea of the essay? _____

_____

_____

4. What facts, examples, or statistics does the author use to support his or her main idea? _____

_____

_____

_____

5. How does the author conclude his or her essay? _____

_____

_____

_____

Save Trees and the Environment by Recycling Newspapers

Recycling newspapers is a way to save trees and our environment. Each week Americans throw out over 200 million newspapers. That equals about 500,000 trees. Although our town has had a recycling program for two years, less than half of our residents bother to recycle newspapers.

This is unfortunate, because recycling newspapers can significantly lessen the burden on our environment. Making paper from recycled paper uses up to 50 percent less energy than making paper from trees. It also reduces related air pollution by 95 percent. Since trees help to filter carbon dioxide and pollutants from the air, saving trees is an important step in reducing overall air pollution.

Everybody can help in the recycling drive. All one needs to do is tie newspapers in bundles and put the bundles out at the curb on the day for recycling.

Recycling will help save trees and the environment. It's everybody's responsibility to get involved.

MINI-LESSON 7:
WRITING FRIENDLY LETTERS

Friendly letters are personal letters written to friends or relatives. Although I don't give grades for friendly letters, I believe students should be taught how to write them.

Procedure:

1. Explain that the purpose of a friendly letter is to tell a friend or relative what has happened recently in the author's life. Friendly letters are informal and are often written in a conversational tone. They should include enough details so that the reader understands what the writer intends. If a writer is responding to a letter she has received, she should attempt to answer any questions the sender has asked.

2. Distribute copies of (or project) the accompanying friendly letter. Read it with your students. Point out the main parts — heading, salutation, body, closing, and signature. Emphasize the punctuation — particularly the commas in the heading and those after the salutation and closing.

3. Tell your students that friendly letters are usually handwritten on letter stationery (although with the increasing use of word processors today, many are typed). Handwriting should be neat, and margins of at least 1" should be left at the top, sides, and bottoms. If more than one sheet is used, page two and following pages should be numbered.

Extensions:

- Give students practice in writing letters. Have students pick a partner and write a friendly letter to him or her.

- Show students how to address envelopes. It's likely that some students have never been shown how to do it correctly.

    - Explain that every envelope must have a mailing address and should have a return address. If the letter cannot be delivered, the return address enables the post office to send it back to the mailer.

    - Note that the mailing address includes the receiver's name, street address (or post office box number), city, state, and ZIP Code. The return address includes the sender's name and complete address.

    - To show your students the proper way to address an envelope, draw the outline of an envelope on the board or an overhead projector and fill in the addresses.

    Mailing Address: Mr. Jimmy Williams, 44 East Street, Hanover, PA 12756. Return Address: Sean Hoover, 129 Deer Run, Peterville, NJ 09423.

Sample Friendly Letter

129 Deer Run
Peterville, NJ 09423
Nov. 10, 1994

Dear Jimmy,

Thanks for your last letter. I was glad to hear from you. Everybody around here still misses you.

Did you watch the last game of the series? I can't believe how it ended. Even though I lost a $5 bet with my Dad, I enjoyed every minute of every game. I suppose I'll always be a baseball fanatic.

Do you think you'll be able to visit during Thanksgiving break? My Mom says you can stay as long as you want. That'll be great. Let me know if you can come.

I'll be looking forward to your next letter.

Your friend,
Sean

MINI-LESSON 8: WRITING BUSINESS LETTERS

Business letters are used to request information, share ideas about business projects, order products or services, or register complaints. Business letters are more formal and briefer than friendly letters. You might mention that query letters are a special kind of business letter in which an author contacts an editor and asks if the editor would be interested in the author's proposed work. (See "Submitting to Magazines" in Section 7.) As with friendly letters, I do not give grades for business letters. Unless students have a reason to write a business letter, it is difficult for them to be genuine in their writing.

Procedure:

1. Explain the purpose of the typical business letter.
2. Distribute copies of (or project) the accompanying sample business letter. Point out the major parts — heading, inside address, salutation, body, closing, and signature.
3. Emphasize that an inside address is included and that a colon follows the salutation.
4. Mention that the business letter may use a block or semiblock form and note the differences on the samples.
5. Tell students that unlike friendly letters, business letters should be typed on 8½" by 11" white paper.

Extension:

- Suggest that students think about products they recently bought. Are there any with which they are particularly pleased or disappointed? If there are, instruct them to write a business letter to the company, informing company representatives of their feelings. Remind students that they will need to have the company's mailing address. (They can probably find it on the product or in the library.)

Sample Business Letter

Semiblock Form

123 Hill Street
Holly Hill, NY 17625
April 3, 1994

Ellis Poster Company
1507 Field Road
Farmingdale, IA 67438

Dear Sir or Madam:

    I would like to order your "Save the Earth" poster, catalogue #873642. Enclosed is $1.95, which includes the cost of postage.

Thank you.

                         Sincerely,

                         Jason Smith

Block Form

123 Hill Street
Holly Hill, NY 17652
April 3, 1994

Ellis Poster Company
1507 Field Road
Farmingdale, IA 67438

Dear Sir or Madam:

I would like to order your "Save the Earth" poster, catalogue #873642. Enclosed is $1.95, which includes the cost of postage.

Thank you.

Sincerely,

Jason Smith

MINI-LESSON 9:
WRITING BOOK REVIEWS

A book review is an in-depth, insightful analysis of a book. A good review explains what the book is about (without giving away any important information) and usually offers the reviewer's opinion. A good source of reviews is the Sunday *New York Times Book Review.* In its book review section, both fiction and nonfiction works are covered. Moreover, while some reviews are lengthy and literary, others are rather short and direct.

The connection between reading and writing is a strong one. Most good writers are good readers. When students read a book to write a review, they are forced to read critically, which will help them to become better readers of their own writing.

Procedure:

1. Explain that a good book review includes the title of the book, the author's name, and the publisher. It may also include the date of publication, the price, and where the book can be obtained.

2. Distribute copies of (or project) the accompanying sample review of *A Wrinkle in Time* by Madeleine L'Engle. Give students a minute or so to read it.

3. Explain that for a review of a fictional work, the reviewer should include an introduction of the plot, a description of the characters, and an outline of the characters' motivations that provide the basis of the story. Any outstanding elements such as quality of writing, fast action, exotic settings, or unusual twists might also be mentioned. The author shouldn't reveal the climax, since others may decide to read the book, but he or she can express an opinion about the ending. Point out that the sample review follows this structure.

4. For nonfiction, explain the scope of the book. The importance of the book, and what it offers, or fails to offer, should be highlighted.

Extension:

• Set up a corner of the room to display book reviews written by your students. This is an excellent way to support both reading and writing.

A Sample Book Review

A Wrinkle in Time
by Madeleine L'Engle (New York: Dell, 1962.)

A reader's first impression of *A Wrinkle in Time* by Madeleine L'Engle will probably be that the story is science fiction. But he or she will soon realize that it is much more. It is a story of mystery, suspense, horror, and love.

Meg Murray, a teenager, can't sleep because of a storm that rages in the night. It's not just the storm that is bothering Meg, though. She has problems fitting in at school, she is convinced that she is not pretty, and she frets that she can't do anything right. On top of all this, her father, a scientist who works for the government, has disappeared.

She goes downstairs where she finds her five-year-old brother Charles Wallace. Most people think that he is a moron, but Charles Wallace has strange and wonderful abilities. A short while later, Meg and Charles Wallace are joined by their mother. (Twin ten-year-old brothers, Sandy and Denny, complete the family. Unlike Meg and Charles Wallace, they are very normal and play a small part in the story.)

Meg, her brother, and mother are interrupted by Mrs. Whatsit, an unusual, unearthly woman. Charles Wallace knows her and greets her warmly, but Meg is suspicious. She thinks Mrs. Whatsit is a tramp.

When Mrs. Whatsit casually mentions that "there is such a thing as a tesseract" (a wrinkle in time), Mrs. Murray is shocked. That was what Mr. Murray had been researching before he disappeared.

This is the beginning of an incredible journey for Meg and Charles Wallace. They soon meet Mrs. Who and Mrs. Which and Calvin O'Keefe, a teenager who, like Charles Wallace, possesses extraordinary powers. Together they journey through wrinkles in time in search of Meg's father. They learn that he is fighting great evil. To help him, the children must confront that evil, too.

Through this confrontation, Meg finds more than her father. She also finds herself.

A Wrinkle in Time is a fine story that is likely to hold any reader's interest.

MINI-LESSON 10:
WRITING MOVIE REVIEWS

Movie reviews are similar to book reviews in basic structure; however, they usually include a discussion of the cinematography with the storyline. Many newspapers contain movie reviews in their TV and movie sections.

Procedure:

1. Explain what a movie review is.

2. Distribute copies of (or project) the accompanying sample review of *The Babe*. Ask students to read it.

3. Explain that reviewers should summarize the plot (without giving away the ending), describe the characters, and offer information about the film's visual impact. Some of the questions they should answer include:

   • Was the action exciting?

   • How interesting or amusing was the film?

   • How believable was the dialogue?

   • How was the acting?

   • If special effects were used, were they believable?

   • Were the costumes and settings realistic?

   • Did the movie have a good sound track?

   Reviewers might also mention the rating of the movie and offer their opinion of whom would be suitable viewers. Since movies offer a message (it may be trivial, but it's there), suggest to your reviewers that they look for a message in the films they watch and include it in their reviews.

Extensions:

   • Include a section of movie reviews in a class magazine.

   • Ask students to bring in movie reviews from newspapers. They should share and discuss the reviews with their peer groups. Caution them to keep the discussion on the way the reviews were written, and not a mere discussion of the movie.

Sample Movie Review

The Babe
A Universal release, written and produced by John Fusco

Everybody knows Babe Ruth. *The Babe* is a sentimental movie that pays respect to Babe Ruth's bigger than life legend. John Goodman plays George Herman Ruth, showing Babe's ready smile and swagger.

The script moves quickly through the Babe's youth, at times sacrificing historical reality for dramatic appeal. Believing that the boy is incorrigible, his parents leave him at an orphanage. Suffering from guilt and rage, the Babe finds an outlet in baseball. It isn't long before he winds up with the Baltimore Orioles. By the time he is traded to Boston, he has learned about cigars, liquor, and women. It is becoming clear that Babe is a complicated man. Shy, sensitive, and prone to being vulgar, all this Babe truly wants is respect.

He finds plenty of that after his sale to the Yankees. In the greatest years of his career, Babe becomes a baseball hero.

The movie follows his success and also his decline. It takes us through his two marriages, the loss of his skills, and his disappointment at not becoming a baseball manager.

Director Arthur Hiller moves the story smoothly through period settings that add realism to the film. In many of the stadium scenes the viewer almost feels that he is in the stands, rooting for the Babe.

Although Goodman plays the Babe with a fine touch, revealing that through much of his life, Babe Ruth was an overgrown boy, he fails to bring to the screen Babe's charisma. After all, this was a man who made baseball the national pastime. But Goodman shouldn't be faulted for this. It's unlikely that anyone can recreate the true Babe Ruth.

The Babe isn't a homerun. It won't please baseball purists, but it's surely worth a triple.

MINI-LESSON 11:
WRITING FICTION

While there are many genres of fiction — mysteries, adventures, westerns, horrors, comedies, and fantasies are just a few examples — all require a plot. This is the action plan of a story. For students to write effective stories, they must understand the elements of a good plot. (For more information on story elements and the role they play in writing fiction, see Mini-lessons 33-39.)

Procedure:

1. Explain that in the most common plot, the lead character has a problem and the story grows around his trying to solve it. The more he tries to solve it, unfortunately, the worse things become. These setbacks are called complications. The lead character keeps running into complications until the story reaches the climax. This is the point where he either solves the problem or he fails.

2. Distribute copies of (or project) the sample plot. Allow time for students to read it.

3. Explain the plot breakdown:

   Problem: Peter wants to ask Sara to the Valentine's Day Dance.

   Complications: His spilling water on her during the science experiment, his dropping her lunch, and his calling her and becoming so nervous that he hangs up.

   Solution: When Sara needs help with science after school, Peter is the only one willing to stay and help her. Because of this they learn that they like each other and Sara agrees to go to the dance with him.

4. Note that this is a happy ending. Sometimes lead characters don't solve their problems. Tragedies often end with lead characters failing.

A Sample Plot

Peter would like to ask Sara to the Valentine's Day Dance. His problem is that Sara hardly knows he's alive. Making the problem worse is Sara's popularity. Being one of the prettiest cheerleaders in the school, Sara is besieged by offers for dates. To gain her attention, Peter does everything he can to impress her. In science class he tries to help her with an experiment, but it backfires and he splashes her with water. At lunch he offers to carry her tray, but he drops it. That night he calls her on the phone to apologize, but he becomes so nervous that he abruptly hangs up. The next day he tries to tell her that they were disconnected because his phone broke, but she doesn't believe him and becomes angry with him. Peter's chances don't look good.

The next day Peter goes to the science lab after school to finish an experiment. He finds Sara there. She is desperately working on an assignment that she needs to get a good grade on her report card. None of her friends was willing to stay and help her. At first Peter hesitates, thinking of how foolish he has been acting. But he decides to help her anyway, because it is the right thing to do. Afterward, Sara realizes that Peter is a nice boy whom she would like to get to know better. When he summons enough courage to ask her to go to the dance, she agrees.

MINI-LESSON 12:
WRITING ADVERTISING

We are constantly bombarded by advertisements. Powerful messages to buy products and services come to us on TV; through the radio; in junk mail, newspapers, and magazines; and on billboards. Almost everywhere we go we find advertisements (or, more accurately, advertisements find us). Since you will probably focus on written advertisements in the writing workshop, you should bring in examples of junk mail, brochures, and ads that appear in newspapers and magazines.

Procedure:

1. Explain that advertising is an important writing form. Every ad is the creation of a writer. Advertisements range from the slickest TV spot selling perfume to the simplest classified. The purpose of every ad is to sell a product, service, cause, or person. Ask your students to volunteer an example of each.

2. Distribute copies of (or project) the accompanying "Advertising Fundamentals."

3. Review the fundamentals with your students.

4. Emphasize that because ad writers always have a limited amount of space or time to get their message across, they make sure that every word is purposeful. Every word must build to the whole to sell.

Extensions:

• Distribute copies of junk mail, brochures, and ads that appear in newspapers or magazines. (A few days in advance of this activity, ask students to bring in examples of advertisements from home.) Also hand out copies of "Advertisement Review." Divide the class into groups of four to six students. Each student should have one ad to review. After reviewing the ad and filling out the worksheet, students are to report to their group members their overall impressions of the ad according to the categories on the worksheet. You may then have each group pick what they feel is the most persuasive ad and have one of the members report about it to the class.

• Suggest that students write advertisements (silly or serious) that will be printed in a class magazine.

Advertising Fundamentals

The average person in the United States is bombarded by thousands of advertisements each week. Ads may be on TV or radio, in newspapers or magazines, on billboards and posters; they may even arrive via mail. Although advertisements vary in content and form, all have common points.

Every advertisement:

Attracts attention through headlines, color, photos, or illustrations. Some ads use only one or two of these devices, others use them all. TV commercials add in music and live action. The best headline catches attention immediately. Ads may show people using or needing a product or service or dedicating themselves to a cause, or may associate the product with an important person, attractive people, wealth, beauty, status, or success.

Arouses interest by promising benefits to the target audience of the ad. Good ads show how purchasing the product or service or accepting the cause or person being advertised can help the targeted individual.

Creates desire by showing the target audience why it needs to accept what the ad is selling. This is done through solid writing that uses strong appeal words and phrases like *best, easy, free, fresh, new, improved, guaranteed, save, inexpensive, help, proven results, money back if not satisfied,* and *full warranty.* Appeals to self-esteem, personal satisfaction, and responsibility are often used by ads that are selling a cause or a person.

Calls for action by telling the target audience to buy now, order today, or make a commitment as soon as possible. Some ads include offers of free gifts or discounts as incentives.

Name _____ Date _____ Class _____

Advertisement Review

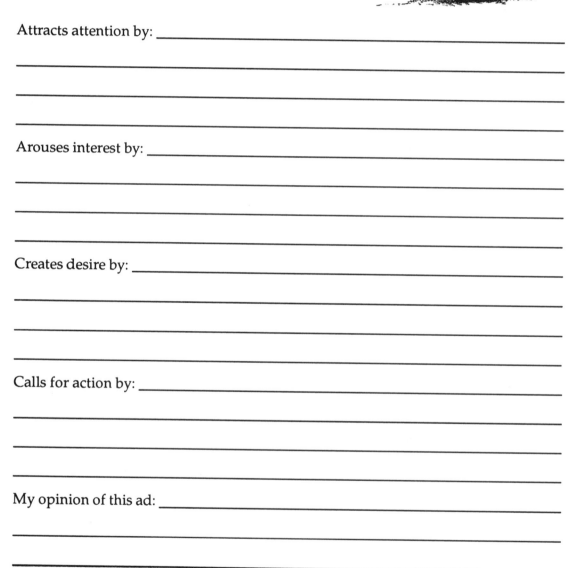

Directions: Review your advertisement and decide how it follows the fundamentals of sound advertising. When you are done, share your findings with your group. Attach your ad to this sheet.

Attracts attention by: _____

_____

_____

_____

Arouses interest by: _____

_____

_____

_____

Creates desire by: _____

_____

_____

_____

Calls for action by: _____

_____

_____

_____

My opinion of this ad: _____

_____

_____

MINI-LESSON 13:
WRITING NONRHYMING POEMS

Many poems don't rhyme. Nonrhyming poems offer students a chance to write poetry without worrying about matching words with the same sounds, thus freeing them to concentrate on ideas and imagery.

There are many excellent collections of poetry from which you can read examples of nonrhyming poems to your students. Two I like are *Rose, Where Did You Get That Red?* by Kenneth Koch (New York: Random House, 1973) and *Poet's Choice*, edited by Paul Engle and Joseph Langland (New York: Time Incorporated, 1966).

Procedure:

1. Explain that most poems do not rhyme. This may be a surprise to some students who have read only rhyming verse.

2. Distribute copies of (or project) the accompanying "Two Student-Written Nonrhyming Poems." Ask students to read them.

3. Note that each of the poems expresses its ideas without rhyme or meter.

4. Point out that poets select their words carefully so that they can evoke strong images in the minds of their readers. Sometimes they will use short lines or one-word lines for emphasis. Note some examples on the poems.

5. Mention that poets sometimes ignore the standard rules of punctuation. They may do this to provide emphasis or as a way to let their ideas stand out in contrast to prose.

Extensions:

- Publish examples of students' poems in a class or school magazine.

- Encourage students to write haiku, cinquain, or other types of nonrhyming poems. (You can easily devote a number of mini-lessons to various poetry formats.)

Two Student-Written Nonrhyming Poems

Morning Song

A new day starts
  With the singing of birds.
Their melodies are light,
  Happy in the coming of the new sun.
The notes arise to the treetops,
  Announcing to the world that a new day has arrived.

Listening to the birds
  I realize I'd rather
Remain in bed
  Than confront the day.

Love Dying

How can you tell
When love's ended?
Is there a sign that says
The End?
Does love stop of a sudden?
Without warning?
Or does it slowly slip
Away and die like a
Flower at the end of its time?
First the richness of its color fades,
Then the sweetness of its nectar dries,
Until, at last,
Its petals wrinkle and fall away and
Turn to dust,
Scattered by the wind?

MINI-LESSON 14:
WRITING RHYMING POEMS

Rhyming poems are likely to be the most familiar to your students. They are very popular and are found in many collections. *Rose, Where Did You Get That Red?* by Kenneth Koch and *Poet's Choice,* edited by Engle and Langland, both noted earlier, are good sources. Another is *Poetry Sampler,* edited by Donald Hall (New York: Franklin Watts, Inc., 1962).

Much of the poetry of Edgar Allan Poe offers fine examples of rhyme and meter. A good source is the *Complete Stories and Poems of Edgar Allan Poe* (Garden City, NY: Doubleday, 1966).

Procedure:

1. Mention that most people are familiar with rhyming poems.
2. Distribute copies of (or project) "Eldorado" by Edgar Allan Poe. Ask students to read it.
3. Point out the rhyme and rhythm of the poem.
4. Share the legend of El Dorado, which was a fabled city of gold thought to exist in the northern part of South America. Spanish, German, and English explorers made several attempts to find the city and its fabulous wealth, but none succeeded.

Extensions:

- Explain that poets use various rhyme patterns. Select examples of some and read them to your students. Some common rhyme patterns for poems that have four-line stanzas include —

  First and second lines rhyme,
  third and fourth lines rhyme.

  First and third lines rhyme,
  second and fourth lines rhyme.

  First and fourth lines rhyme,
  second and third lines rhyme.

- To help your students write rhyming poems, suggest that they develop rhyming word lists. A rhyming word list is generated by taking a word such as snow and listing other words that rhyme with it. Put snow on the board or an overhead projector and have students offer words that rhyme with it:

  Snow — know, no, grow, glow, flow, whoa, so, doe, go, throw, blow, slow, hoe, ho, bow, crow, low

- Discuss the use of a rhyming dictionary. Point out that most of these books list sounds, after which words that rhyme with the sound are offered. If you have a rhyming dictionary available, encourage students to use it.

- Publish students' poems in a class or school magazine.

- Hold a class poetry reading session.

- Encourage students to write limericks.

Eldorado

by Edgar Allan Poe

Gaily bedight,
A gallant knight,
In sunshine and in shadow,
Had journeyed long,
Singing a song,
In search of Eldorado.

But he grew old—
This knight so bold—
And o'er his heart a shadow
Fell as he found
No spot of ground
That looked like Eldorado

And, as his strength
Failed him at length,
He met a pilgrim shadow—
"Shadow," said he,
"Where can it be—
This land of Eldorado?"

"Over the Mountains
Of the Moon,
Down the Valley of the Shadow,
Ride, boldly ride,"
The Shade replied,—
"If you seek for Eldorado."

MINI-LESSON 15:
WRITING PLAYS_____

Plays are a form of literature designed to be performed on a stage. Thus the playwright must consider the visual appeal of her writing along with her words. She must plan carefully what she wishes to say as well as how it will be said.

Procedure:

1. Hand out copies of (or project) the accompanying "Parts of a Play" and review it with your students.

2. Depending on the type of problem and number of obstacles and complications, a play can be relatively short, a scene or two, or quite lengthy with several acts and scenes. No matter how long or complicated, however, the basic structure of most plays is the same.

3. Hand out copies of the sample play beginning, "Ghost Hunt." (*Note:* This is not the structure that professional playwrights use, but it works well for students.) Briefly point out the format on the sample.

   a. Plays are organized into acts and scenes, which divide the play into sections.

   b. The setting is described at the beginning of scenes, and AT RISE relates the action as the curtain goes up.

   c. In dialogue, the names of characters are capitalized and followed by a colon.

   d. Brief stage directions and descriptions may be included with dialogue and are set in parentheses, but detailed stage directions or descriptions are usually separated from dialogue and written in parentheses.

   e. A line is skipped between characters.

   f. The word CURTAIN is used to end a scene.

Extensions:

- Produce some of the plays your students write.

- Stage formal readings or rehearsals of plays your students have written. (The actors don't have to memorize lines, and costumes and sets are unnecessary.)

The Parts of a Play

Most plays are built around the following parts:

Opening — A problem is revealed (or alluded to) and background information is supplied.

Plan — The lead character(s) try to solve the problem and reach a goal.

Obstacles and complications — Events, situations, and dilemmas block the characters in their attempts to solve the problem.

Climax — The characters solve the problem or they fail. Based on either solving or failing to solve the problem, the goal is reached or not reached.

Ghost Hunt

CHARACTERS: Todd, fifteen years old
                   Cindy, fifteen years old
                   Billy, fourteen years old

ACT I

Scene 1

SETTING: A garage in which a variety of tools and lawn implements are scattered about. It is night and outside the window it is dark. A long workbench with three knapsacks loaded with flashlights, cameras, lanterns, and other equipment stretches against the back wall.

AT RISE: Todd, Billy, and Cindy are at the workbench. Todd is checking one of the knapsacks. When he is satisfied with its contents, he slips a thermos in.

TODD (turning to others): That's it. We're set.

BILLY: You may be set, but I'm not sure I am.

CINDY: You're not afraid, are you? (Skeptically) You don't really think we're going to find any ghosts in old man Fraser's house.

BILLY: People say it's been haunted for years. The place gives me the creeps.

TODD (confidently): If there are ghosts there, we're going to prove it.

(He pulls out a camera from his knapsack and holds it up. He is quite pleased with it.)

TODD: The shutter speed on this little baby is fast enough to catch anything on film.

BILLY: Even ghosts?

TODD: Even ghosts.

CINDY: Well, you've photographed just about everything else. Why not add some ghosts to your albums?

TODD (grinning): You got it. Let's go . . .

MINI-LESSON 16:
SCREENPLAYS

Screenplays, sometimes referred to as scripts, are stories written for the movies or television. There are many sources for formats for screenplays. One I refer to is *The Elements of Screenwriting: A Guide for Film and Television Writers* by Irwin R. Blacker (New York: Macmillan, 1986).

Procedure:

1. Explain what a screenplay is.
2. Hand out copies of (or project) the accompanying sample beginning of the screenplay, "The Test." Instruct students to read it.
3. Point out the special format:
   a. Screenplays begin with a title.
   b. Acts divide the screenplay into parts.
   c. Individual scenes are numbered on the right-hand side of the script. Emphasize that a scene is a segment of the story that takes place in a particular setting.
   d. The names of characters are capitalized on the script. Dialogue appears under the speaker's name.
   e. Dialogue and any descriptions are single-spaced with double-spacing between words of different characters and scenes.

Extensions:

- For students who show particular interest in writing screenplays, hand out copies of "Screenplay Vocabulary."

- With the aid of a video camera, produce and film some of the scripts your students write.

Screenplay Format

The Test

ACT I

FADE IN:
EXT., FRONT YARD OF SCHOOL   1

    The camera shows the front yard of a modern, suburban school. Grass on the front court is trimmed; nicely pruned shrubs dot the area. Students are arriving to begin the day. It is bright and sunny. Three teenage friends, PETER JACKSON, TOM REYNOLDS, and DEBBIE WILLIAMS are walking together toward the school.

The camera moves in on the three teenagers.   2

DEBBIE
(sighing, worried)

I don't know how I'm going to pass that history test today.

PETER

Yeah...old lady Skinner's tests are murder. I need a good grade or I'm grounded.

TOM
(smiling)

What's passing worth to you?

PETER

What do you mean?

TOM takes a crumpled sheet of paper from his pocket.

DEBBIE

What's that?

TOM

Nothing much . . . just the answers to the test . . .

Screenplay Vocabulary

Writers of movies and TV programs use a special vocabulary in developing their scripts.

angle on   what the camera sees; the viewpoint of the camera.

back to   a return to the previous scene.

close-up   a close shot.

cut to   a switch from the viewpoint of one camera to another, often employed to change scenes.

director   the person who supervises the filming of a screenplay.

dissolve   the gradual disappearing of one scene to be replaced with another.

dolly   the moving of the camera toward or away from a scene.

ext.   abbreviation for *exterior*, used when a scene takes place outside.

fade in   the gradual appearing of a scene.

fade out   the gradual disappearing of a scene.

favoring   a shot that focuses on one character in a group.

insert   a shot of something put into a scene, for example, a letter or a map.

int.   abbreviation for *interior*, used when a scene takes place inside.

long shot   a camera shot of an entire scene.

pan   a camera shot that moves from side to side.

pov   a shot taken from a character's point of view, showing what the character sees.

producer   the person who plans, coordinates, and supervises all phases of the making of a motion picture or TV show.

vo   abbreviation for *voice over*, a scene in which a character's voice is heard but he or she is not seen.

Mini-lessons for the Art of Writing

MINI-LESSON 17:
EFFECTIVE LEADS

The lead is the beginning of any piece. If the lead is not interesting, it is unlikely that the rest of the piece will be read. Good writers know how important the lead is, and many spend more time on it proportionately than they do on the other parts of their work.

Procedure:

1. Explain that every lead must "hook" the reader immediately. A good lead captures the reader's interest, introduces the subject or problem, and carries the reader into the following material.

2. Mention that some leads may be a few sentences, while others may run several paragraphs. The "leads" of books may last several pages or fill an entire chapter.

3. Distribute copies of (or project) the accompanying "Leads" and discuss the information. Emphasize the many ways that authors write leads.

4. Suggest that students write three, four, or more leads and then pick the best one for their piece. Students may also read their leads to a partner or peer group and ask their peers to help them decide on the best lead.

5. Offer these tips for students who have trouble writing a lead:

    a. They should make sure that the focus of the piece is clear.

    b. Sometimes the second paragraph of a piece makes a better lead than the first.

    c. For those times when ideas for leads just don't come, students should meet with a partner or peer group, tell peers what they intend to write, and ask for suggestions of possible leads. Stress that the author must be the one to make the final decision about his or her lead.

Extensions:

- Distribute copies of (or project) the accompanying "Sample Leads." Instruct your students to read the four possible leads of an article about how to study effectively for tests. Point out the differences between the leads:

    - Lead 1 uses an example.

    - Lead 2 relies on a quote.

    - Lead 3 asks the reader a question.

    - Lead 4 starts with a statement of the problem.

    Note that there are many other possible leads for the article. Divide your students into peer groups and have them brainstorm some other leads.

- Suggest that students review the leads of various articles and stories and identify the method the author used. They may refer to the handout "Leads." Students should share their findings in peer groups.

Leads

Whatever type of lead you choose for a piece, it must:

- Capture the reader's interest.
- Introduce your subject or problem.
- Move smoothly into the body of your piece.

Here are some ways you can write leads.

For Nonfiction

- State a problem.
- Use an interesting quotation.
- Ask the reader a direct question.
- Offer an interesting or unusual fact.
- Offer an alarming or surprising statistic.
- Relate a compelling anecdote, or a joke.
- Offer an exaggeration of a common situation.

For Fiction

- Show a problem or conflict characters have.
- Show action (in which a character is performing a task) that is related to a problem.
- Start with dialogue in which characters are talking about a problem.
- Create a sense of foreboding; something important (the problem) is about to happen.
- Depict a humorous situation.

Sample Leads

There are many ways to write leads for your pieces. Following are four possible leads for an article about how to study effectively for tests.

Lead 1

Jason is a typical high school junior. Last night he was studying for a major history test. Feeling that music relaxes him, he put on the stereo and hit the books. After two hours—during which he treated himself to some snacks and his favorite TV show—he decided that he had studied enough. After all, he had put in two hours.

The next day Jason bombed. Why? He doesn't know how to study effectively.

Lead 2

"Students fail tests because they don't know how to study," says Ed Harmon, a high school history teacher. Harmon's statement is echoed by teachers throughout the country.

Lead 3

Do you know how to study for tests? If you answered yes, you are in the minority. Most students don't know how to study for tests effectively.

Lead 4

Test-taking is a major activity in American schools. It is also one of the most anxiety-causing. The reason for this comes down to a simple fact—most students don't know how to study for tests.

MINI-LESSON 18:
ORGANIZATION FOR NONFICTION WRITING_____

In writing, good organization results in a smooth flow of main ideas and details that carry the reader along and build to a whole. Just as a house is constructed one brick at a time, an article or story is written by building one idea on top of another.

Procedure:

1. Explain that nonfiction writing is most often organized in a *chronological* or *logical* manner.

2. In a *chronological pattern,* ideas or events are usually arranged in the sequence in which they occurred. For example, what happens first in time appears first, what happens second appears second, and what happens third appears third, building to a conclusion. The chronological pattern is common for personal narratives and fiction.

3. In a *logical pattern,* ideas are arranged in some systematic way. A description of a place, for instance, might be organized from left to right, inside to outside, or up to down. Another logical pattern is arranging ideas in order from least to most important, or from most to least important.

4. Caution students that whatever way they organize their information, their ideas must be supported with facts, examples, or statistics.

5. Distribute copies of (or project) the accompanying "Vanishing Ozone." Instruct students to read it. Note that after the opening, ideas are presented that support the article's main purpose, which is to explain what ozone is, how the ozone layer is being destroyed by chlorofluorocarbons (CFCs), and what can be done to stop the destruction.

Extensions:

- Suggest that students look for organizational patterns in articles that they read.

- Give students a collection of facts and have them work together in small groups to organize the facts into a report.

- For additional information see "Organizing Writing" in Section 3.

Vanishing Ozone

The ozone layer is a thin part of the Earth's atmosphere. It is important because it protects every living thing on Earth from the sun's harmful ultraviolet radiation. Without the ozone layer, human skin cancer rates would rise, crop yields would go down, and an increase in genetic mutations could occur. Yet every day more of the ozone layer is being destroyed by manmade chemicals.

Ozone is a special molecule of oxygen that has three atoms. It forms naturally in sunlight. Most of the ozone layer's destruction is caused by gases called chlorofluorocarbons (also known as CFCs). These gases are found in many common products. Freon, for example, a coolant used in refrigerators and air conditioners, is a CFC. CFCs were also used in many aerosol spray cans. Although the federal government banned CFCs from most aerosol cans in 1978, researchers haven't been able to find substitutes for all of them yet. CFCs are still used to make some types of polystyrene, which is used in packing boxes to prevent breakage, in insulation, and in some types of coolers.

In whatever way they are used, when CFCs escape to the atmosphere, they rise to the ozone layer and begin damaging it. Sunlight breaks the CFCs down and then they react with ozone molecules, destroying them.

You can help save the ozone layer by following some simple steps. First, make sure that your air conditioners and refrigerators are working properly. If they are not cooling efficiently, it might be because of a leak in freon. Have the unit repaired by a trained technician so that the freon and its CFCs will not escape to the air. You should also avoid buying aerosol spray cans that contain CFCs. Many cans list their ingredients. Look for phrases like "Ozone friendly" or "Contains no CFCs." Finally, when using foam insulation, make sure no CFCs are present and try to buy products that are not packed in polystyrene that may contain CFCs.

Because it blocks the sun's harmful rays from reaching the Earth's surface, the ozone layer is crucial for life. Loss of the ozone layer would affect life throughout the world.

MINI-LESSON 19:
WRITING CONCLUSIONS FOR NONFICTION PIECES_____

Many students (and professional writers, too!) have trouble knowing when to end a piece. Writing after a piece is "done," however, stretches it out and weakens the impression it would otherwise have on the reader. Some students keep writing in the hope that if they write more you will give them a better grade. In either case it's like the guest who stays well past the time everyone else is ready to call it a night. Just as that guest takes the glow off the evening, a weak conclusion detracts from the writing that comes before it.

Procedure:

1. Explain that a good conclusion flows naturally out of the body of the piece. Tell your students that once they have gotten across all the ideas they wish to share in their piece, it is time to conclude. Continuing to write after that will only repeat ideas or include ideas that don't belong.

2. Distribute copies of (or project) "Vanishing Ozone" from Mini-lesson 18. Instruct students to read the article and focus on the conclusion.

3. Explain these two common methods of concluding a piece.

   a. A conclusion may be a mere summary of the main ideas of a piece. While this may be acceptable for writers who are still uncertain of themselves, it is not the best conclusion.

   b. A better way to conclude a piece is to leave the reader with a final thought that ties together the main ideas. This is the method used in "Vanishing Ozone." Note how the main point is restated and the reader is left with a final idea to ponder.

Extension:

- Encourage students to read magazine articles to see how the authors concluded their work. They should share their findings with members of their peer groups and discuss the ways authors conclude their work. In this way students will be exposed to different kinds of conclusions.

MINI-LESSON 20: CONCISENESS

Most of the best writing is concise. Brevity helps writing to flow smoothly and makes it easier for the reader to comprehend the author's ideas. Everything becomes clearer; less becomes more.

Procedure:

1. Explain that to write concisely requires eliminating all unnecessary words. This is difficult even for professional authors.

2. Suggest that when they finish a draft, students ask an editing partner to read it carefully and underline every word, phrase, and sentence that the editor feels might be eliminated. The final decision on this rests with the author, but the identification of possible places to cut is the first step to reaching conciseness.

3. Distribute copies of (or project) "Cutting Clutter." Briefly go over the examples that show how clutter can be eliminated and concise writing achieved. Emphasize that these are only some examples and that good writers are always on the lookout for ways to make their writing concise.

Cutting Clutter

Good writing is concise. The author tries to eliminate all unnecessary words, phrases, and sentences. Following are examples of wordy phrases with concise alternatives. Look for phrases like these in your writing and revise them.

Cluttered Phrase	Alternative
great in size	great
twenty in number	twenty
personal friend	friend
with regard to	about
that there	that
all of a sudden	suddenly
at the present time	now
by means of	by
completely filled	filled
during the time that	while
foreign imports	imports
for the purpose of	for
in relation to	about
doctor by profession	doctor
order up	order
referred to as	called
in view of the fact that	as
with the exception of	except
thought to him- or herself	thought
until such a time	until
prior to the start of	before
seems to be	is
entirely finished	finished
red in color	red
on the subject of	about

MINI-LESSON 21:
*AVOIDING INTENSIFIERS AND QUALIFIERS*_____

Intensifiers and qualifiers can fill a piece with useless words and phrases that obscure ideas; ironically, they may actually weaken rather than strengthen an author's points.

Procedure:

1. Explain that writers may use intensifiers and qualifiers in the hope of adding emphasis to their words. Strong writing, however, doesn't need them.

2. Offer these examples of intensifiers and qualifiers by writing them on the board or on an overhead projector:

Intensifiers	*Qualifiers*
really	in a sense
very	sort of
so	kind of
	a bit
	seemingly
	somewhat

3. "Very" and "really," for instance, are unnecessary to just about any sentence. Suppose a day is cloudy. How much cloudier must it be to be "very" cloudy? Cloudy is cloudy. "Really" in most cases is simply a waste word. It offers no additional meaning to a word it modifies. Is there a difference between good and "really" good?

4. Explain that a thing is never "sort of," "kind of," or "in a sense." It is or it isn't. For example, a day may be partly cloudy, but it is not "sort of" cloudy. "Sort of" in that example is vague. It doesn't convey the idea clearly.

5. "A bit" or "somewhat" means a part of something. Yet we often use these qualifiers in sentences like—"All it takes is a bit of luck to win a lottery." "A bit" doesn't add to the sentence. After all, how much is "a bit" of luck?

6. Mention that intensifiers and qualifiers can weaken writing. Offer these examples:

   "She was a very lovely woman" sounds weaker than "She was a lovely woman."

   "He was really angry" sounds weaker than "He was angry."

   (Note that these guidelines for using intensifiers and qualifiers may not extend to dialogue. People use them all the time in normal speech.)

7. Emphasize that intensifiers and qualifiers slip into writing easily. Authors must proofread their work carefully to eliminate them from their pieces.

MINI-LESSON 22:
ACTIVE AND PASSIVE CONSTRUCTIONS

Good writers use active rather than passive constructions. Active constructions are forceful and add clarity to writing. Passive constructions are weak.

Here is a sentence using an active verb: "Jim punched Joe." It is strong and direct and paints a clear image. Compare it to its passive counterpart. "Joe was punched by Jim." This is wordy and less vivid. Writing that is filled with passive constructions plods. Too much of it makes writing flat.

Procedure:

1. Put the following examples of active and passive constructions on the board or an overhead projector and discuss them with your students.

    The mother carried her baby. (*active*)
    The baby was carried by her mother. (*passive*)

    Jeff smiled at Kim. (*active*)
    Kim was smiled at by Jeff. (*passive*)

    Point out that although the verbs are the same, the construction of the sentence is different.

2. Mention that passive constructions also include uses of the verb "to be." Share this example:

    It rained all night. (*active*)
    It was a rainy night. (*passive*)

    Explain that passive constructions of the verb "to be" can often be rewritten using stronger action words, as in taking "rainy," an adjective, and using its verb form, "rained."

3. Point out the wordiness and loss of energy in the passive sentences compared to the active ones. Active constructions help readers to visualize action easier.

Extension:

*   Suggest that students take one of their pieces, read through it, and circle any passive constructions they find. They should then revise the passive constructions, making them active.

MINI-LESSON 23:
CHOOSING STRONG VERBS FOR WRITING_____

Along with choosing active constructions, encourage your students to select strong, precise verbs. Rather than verbs that rely on adverbs to help the reader see the action, good writers pick verbs that can stand alone.

Procedure:

1. Write the following examples of verbs on the board or an overhead projector.

   walked unsteadily—staggered
   walked softly—tiptoed
   yelled loudly—shouted
   punched furiously—pummeled
   held tightly—clutched
   said softly—whispered
   beat wildly—pounded

2. Explain that while the verbs, combined with the adverbs on the left are acceptable, the verbs on the right are precise and forceful. They draw a clear image in the reader's mind and help to make writing more concise.

Extension:

- Suggest that students proofread one of their pieces specifically for instances where they have used adverbs to describe verbs. They should try to replace those verbs with precise, forceful ones.

MINI-LESSON 24:
WRITING EFFECTIVE TRANSITIONS

Transitions are words and phrases that link ideas. They help writing to flow smoothly by forming bridges that enable the reader to move easily from one idea to another. Without effective transitions writing becomes rough and choppy as the switch between ideas is abrupt. The reader is jarred, and the coherence of the piece is shattered.

Procedure:

1. Explain the importance of transitions.

2. Distribute copies of (or project) the accompanying "Transition Sample," which is the beginning of an article on nonverbal communication.

3. Instruct students to read the first version, which is missing an important transition. Ask students to find where a transition is needed. Tell them to read the revised version that includes the missing transition. It is in paragraph 3. In the first version, starting that paragraph with "A smile communicates happiness or pleasure" is an abrupt shift from the description of head gestures. The revision, "Like the head, the face also can be used for communication," carries the main idea of the previous paragraph into the following one, bridging the gap between them. The transition tells the reader that the article has now shifted to a description of facial gestures. It helps the article to flow smoothly.

Extensions:

- Explain that, along with the carryover of ideas to make transitions, writers also use special words and phrases to link ideas. Put the following words on the board or an overhead projector:

after	but	in addition to
also	during	instead of
although	earlier	just as
at last	finally	later
before	for example	rather than
beyond	however	therefore

- Mention that these are some of the more common words used for transitions and that there are many others. Any word or phrase that links ideas can be used.

- Suggest that as they read stories or articles, students look for transitions and see how authors construct them.

Transition Sample

Nonverbal Communication

Version 1

When most people think of communication, they think of talking. But people can speak nonverbally, too, through various gestures. Head, facial, hand, and body gestures can send clear messages to others.

The most common head gestures are the shake and nod. When a person shakes his head, he moves his head horizontally from side to side. The message sent is no. The head nod, however, in which the head moves up and down, means yes. Since the head nod is found in every culture of the world, some psychologists believe that it is an inborn gesture.

A smile communicates happiness or pleasure. A frown expresses sadness or anger. The eyes also are used to communicate. When a person is frustrated, he will often roll his eyes upward. A wink, on the other hand, expresses secrecy. It may affirm something that two people know that others present don't know. It may be an expression of fondness, or it may be a greeting when verbal communication is inappropriate.

Version 2

When most people think of communication, they think of talking. But people can speak nonverbally, too, through various gestures. Head, facial, hand, and body gestures can send clear messages to others.

The most common head gestures are the shake and nod. When a person shakes his head, he moves his head horizontally from side to side. The message sent is no. The head nod, however, in which the head moves up and down, means yes. Since the head nod is found in every culture of the world, some psychologists believe that it is an inborn gesture.

Like the head, the face also can be used for communication. A smile communicates happiness or pleasure. A frown expresses sadness or anger. The eyes also are used to communicate. When a person is frustrated, he will often roll his eyes upward. A wink, on the other hand, expresses secrecy. It may affirm something that two people know that others present don't know. It may be an expression of fondness, or it may be a greeting when verbal communication is inappropriate.

MINI-LESSON 25:
DEVELOPING IMAGERY

Imagery refers to the pictures that readers see in their minds as they read. Good images are created by using specific details that appeal to the senses and make a dominant impression.

Procedure:

1. Explain what imagery is.

2. Distribute copies of (or project) the accompanying sample, "Returning to the Beach." Ask students to read it, then point out the details that build the images, for example:

    . . . breathed deeply of the salty air . . .

    . . . warm sand scrunching beneath my feet and pushing up between my toes.

    . . . The breeze . . . was cool.

    . . . cries of the gulls . . .

3. Emphasize that strong imagery is built on an appeal to the senses (sight, touch, taste, hearing, and smell). Details should be specific and concrete. Offer these examples:

    instead of flower — yellow tulip

    instead of strong smell — pungent odor of garlic

    instead of rain — cold, December rain

    instead of sound of the horn — shrill blast of the horn

    instead of great tasting cake — sweet, chocolate cake

Extension:

- Explain that the ability to write strong imagery comes largely from being a good observer of the world. Suggest that students train themselves to be good observers. Whenever they are at an event, they should look for the details that impress their senses. Distribute copies of "Sense and Image," which students can use as a guide to becoming keen observers of the life around them. After completing the sheet, they may wish to discuss their impressions with members of a peer group.

Returning to the Beach

I hadn't been to the beach in several months. The moment I stepped out of the car I realized how I had missed it.

As I breathed deeply of the salty air, I felt invigorated and renewed. Slipping off my shoes, I walked toward the surf, warm sand scrunching beneath my feet and pushing up between my toes.

The breeze coming off the ocean was cool. That was not surprising in late June, but the sun was hot and high, a sign of summer. The cries of the nearby gulls were soothing, for they reminded me of the many summers I had spent here.

Sense and Image

Directions: Select a place for observation. Some places you might consider include a park, a baseball game, the school cafeteria at lunch time, or your backyard. Observe the details of this place, and record how your senses are stimulated.

Sight: _____

_____

_____

Touch: _____

_____

_____

Hearing: _____

_____

_____

Smell: _____

_____

_____

Taste: _____

_____

_____

MINI-LESSON 26:
TONE

The tone an author uses in a piece reflects his or her attitude toward the material. For example, the sentence, "That's fine," can have different meanings depending on the context in which it is used. It may be said matter-of-factly, sarcastically, or with sympathy. Tone in writing is similar to tone in speaking. Often it communicates just as much as words.

Procedure:

1. Explain what tone is.

2. Explain that the best tone for a piece is one that is appropriate for the material and audience.

3. Note that tone can be formal, tragic, angry, kindly, cheerful, sarcastic, personal, or impersonal. It can reflect the entire range of human emotions. The tone of a how-to article, for example, should be simple and straightforward, while the tone of a comedy piece should be playful and light.

4. Write the following examples of tone on the board or an overhead projector:

    a. Sara's little sister always seems to hang out with Sara and her friends. (*understanding tone*)

    b. Sara's little sister is a nuisance; she's always bothering Sara and her friends. (*cruel tone*)

    c. The government must enact the appropriate legislation now. (*impatient tone*)

    d. The government should take the lead by passing the appropriate legislation. (*moderate tone*)

Extensions:

- Suggest that students try to identify the tone in articles and stories they read.

- If a student writes a piece with a distinctive tone, have that student read the piece for author's chair. Point out how the tone fits the piece and supports the author's intention.

MINI-LESSON 27:
COMPARING AND CONTRASTING_____

Authors use comparing and contrasting to bring out similarities and differences between things. Although the words compare and contrast are often used together, they have different meanings. A comparison examines similarities; a contrast looks at differences.

Procedure:

1. Explain the meanings of comparison and contrast.

2. Explain that comparison and contrast can be used in both fiction and nonfiction. Whenever an author describes similarities or differences between things, he or she is using the technique of comparison and contrast.

3. Note that comparing and contrasting are excellent methods of showing details. They help to paint clear images.

4. Distribute copies of (or project) the accompanying "Comparing and Contrasting — Nonfiction." Instruct your students to read the two examples. Briefly discuss them.

5. Note that there are two ways to compare or contrast.

    a. The author describes the first idea, event, situation, or character completely. He then describes the second and compares or contrasts it with the first.

    b. The author takes one point from each idea, event, situation, or character and compares or contrasts them directly. He then compares or contrasts a second point, then a third, and so on.

    Note that either method is good. However, an author should be consistent with whichever method he chooses and not switch back and forth.

Extension:

- Distribute copies of (or project) "Comparing and Contrasting — Fiction." Have students read the two examples. Discuss them briefly.

Comparing and Contrasting—Nonfiction

Following are two paragraphs of an article about Earth and Venus. Read the paragraphs and note how the planets are compared and contrasted.

Comparing

Venus and Earth are often called sister planets. They have much in common. They are inner planets, Venus being the second planet from the sun and the Earth being the third. Both are almost the same size and have a similar mass and density. Both are composed mostly of rock and iron and possess well-defined land masses. Recent observations indicate that the continents of Venus shift as do the continents of Earth, leading to periodic volcanic eruptions and Venusquakes.

Contrasting

However, the similarities soon end. Just like sisters who don't get along, Earth and Venus have many distinct features. While the average surface temperature of the Earth is about 59 degrees Fahrenheit, the average surface temperature of Venus is near 900 degrees Fahrenheit, hot enough to melt lead. Unlike Earth's atmosphere, which is composed mostly of nitrogen and oxygen, with traces of gases like carbon dioxide, Venus's atmosphere is almost all carbon dioxide. Since carbon dioxide traps the heat of the sun, Venus is an example of a runaway greenhouse effect. Once Venus was thought to be much like Earth, but now astronomers know that it is very different than our own planet.

Comparing and Contrasting—
Fiction

Comparing

It was obvious to Laurie that Tim was John's younger brother. They had the same blonde hair, gray eyes, and quick smiles. Both were tall and had the rugged good looks of boys who enjoyed the outdoors.

(By comparing Tim to John, the author paints a clear physical description of him.)

Contrasting

Tara was unlike her sister Jill. When Jill was happy, Tara was moody. Whereas Jill always seemed to be smiling, Tara wore a constant frown. Even their hair and complexions were different. Jill had light hair and green eyes, while Tara's dark hair and eyes were striking in their utter lack of color.

(By contrasting the two sisters, both are characterized and shown to be quite different.)

MINI-LESSON 28:
AVOIDING CLICHÉS

Clichés are expressions that have been used so often in writing and speaking that they are familiar. That familiarity tarnishes writing. It steals freshness from an author's words, detracts from style, and ruins originality. Clichés, which slip into writing easily, should always be revised.

Procedure:

1. Distribute copies of "Clichés" and review the list with your students. Suggest that they retain the list in their writing folders and refer to it periodically. This will help them to become aware of cliché phrases. Note that this is only a partial list and that they can add to it.

2. Explain that clichés undermine style and freshness.

3. Emphasize that clichés should always be rewritten. Model how that can be done by writing the following examples on the board or an overhead projector.

   It didn't take Tom long to realize that the <u>job was easier said than done</u>.
   It didn't take Tom long to realize that the job was harder than he had thought.

   She <u>sighed in relief</u>.
   She sighed, relieved.

   Rachel was <u>as busy as a bee</u>.
   Rachel was busy.

4. In the first two examples, the clichés are eliminated and the ideas are expressed through revision. In the third, the cliché is eliminated by simply cutting unnecessary words.

5. Note that if a phrase comes to mind easily, or if it sounds familiar, it is likely to be a cliché.

6. Mention that even professional authors have trouble keeping clichés off their pages. It takes careful editing to find them.

Clichés

Clichés are phrases that have been used so much in writing and speaking that they are familiar to readers. Because they are familiar, they make writing stale and boring. Following are some common clichés. Revise them whenever you find them in your writing.

add insult to injury

green with envy

long arm of the law

depths of despair

at death's door

one in a million

writing on the wall

to the bitter end

in a jiffy

bury the hatchet

weigh a ton

accidents will happen

white as a ghost

break the ice

in the same boat

heart skipped a beat

sighed in relief

easier said than done

grinning from ear to ear

in this day and age

few and far between

word to the wise

bite off more than you can chew

not a second too soon

heart on his (her) sleeve

on cloud nine

weary bones

it's in the bag

cried her eyes out

beyond a shadow of a doubt

calm before the storm

stopped dead in his (her) tracks

once in a lifetime

raining cats and dogs

busy as a bee

to make a long story short

MINI-LESSON 29:
CONDUCTING INTERVIEWS

Interviews can be an important source of information. Although most people associate interviews with nonfiction writing, interviews can also provide excellent information for stories.

Procedure:

1. Explain that interviews can provide authors with firsthand information that they may not be able to obtain elsewhere.

2. Mention that interviews with people who are experts on a subject, or who have personal experience with it, can provide interesting quotes that can highlight an author's writing.

3. Explain that effective interviews are the result of several factors. Distribute copies of the accompanying "Guide to Great Interviews" and review these factors with your students.

Extensions:

- Encourage students to interview people who can provide information on topics the students are writing about.

- Suggest that students work with a partner and conduct interviews of each other. After gathering information, students write biographical sketches of their partners. Collect the pieces and publish them in a class book.

Guide to Great Interviews

Interviews can provide authors with information that might be hard or impossible to find elsewhere. Every good interview is a result of several factors:

1. Before attempting to interview anyone on a topic, you must understand the topic. Collect background information.

2. Think of people who can give you the information you need. For example, if you are writing a piece on a fitness plan a person can follow at home, a gym teacher or athletic coach might be good choices for interviews.

3. Think of questions you'd like to ask during the interview. Use questions that encourage explanations. Don't ask: "Is exercise good for a person?" The answer will be a simple yes. Instead ask: "What benefits can a person get from exercise?"

4. Be alert to the answers you receive. They can lead to more questions. If you are not sure about an answer, politely ask for clarification.

5. Take notes or use a tape recorder. If you use a recorder, first ask if the person you are speaking with minds being taped. Some people do. If you use a recorder, make sure it is working properly and that you have an extra set of batteries.

   If you take notes, don't try to write everything down. You'll never be able to. Write down key points. Inventing your own shorthand is helpful. For example, *Mr. Smith* is S, *jogging* is jog, *exercise* is ex, and *and* is +. Such codes will speed your note taking.

6. When you want to quote the person, be sure to use his or her exact words. In your piece, put those words in quotation marks.

7. Don't stretch the interview out longer than necessary. Once you have your information, recheck important facts and thank the person. You might also write a thank-you note a few days later.

MINI-LESSON 30:
USING FIGURES OF SPEECH (SIMILES, METAPHORS, AND PERSONIFICATION)

Figures of speech can enhance style and make ideas distinct. Similes and metaphors make comparisons; personification gives nonhuman things or ideas human qualities. When used properly, figures of speech can elevate a piece from the ordinary to the outstanding.

Procedure:

1. Explain that similes, metaphors, and personification are known as figures of speech.
2. Distribute copies of (or project) the accompanying "Figures of Speech."
3. Explain that similes make comparisons using the words *like, as,* or *than.* Instruct students to read the three examples of similes on the reproducible. Point out the comparisons.
4. Explain that metaphors make comparisons without using *like, as,* or *than.* Have students read the two examples. Point out the comparisons.
5. Explain that personification permits authors to give human qualities to animals, plants, things, and ideas. Have students read the three examples, then point out the personifications.
6. Encourage students to use figures of speech in their writing.

Extension:

- Suggest that students look for figures of speech in their reading. They should study how authors use similes, metaphors, and personification, for this will help them to use figures of speech in their writing.

Figures of Speech

Authors use figures of speech to compare ideas and create strong images. Figures of speech include similes, metaphors, and personification.

Similes

Similes use *like, as,* or *than* to make comparisons.

>Her eyes twinkled *like* the stars.
>His brooding eyes were dark *as* night.
>He was craftier *than* a fox.

Metaphors

Metaphors make comparisons without using the signaling words *like, as* or *than*.

>The mountain range was a wall blocking them from the fertile lands to the south.
>The boxer was a true warrior.

Personification

Personification gives human qualities to nonhuman things or ideas.

>The creatures of the night have their own songs.
>Even the sky wept.
>Two giant boulders stood guard at the entrance of the secret cave.

MINI-LESSON 31:
USING ONOMATOPOEIA

Onomatopoeia is the use of words that sound like the things they name. Because they appeal to the sense of sound, onomatopoeic words can evoke clear, strong images.

Procedure:

1. Explain what onomatopoeia is.

2. Ask your students to listen for the sounds as you read these following examples:

    The bee *buzzed* lazily through the garden, stopping at each flower in search of pollen.

    Note that "buzzed" sounds like a bee and helps the reader/listener to see that bee in his or her imagination.

    The smoke detector *blared* at 2 A.M., shocking John awake.

    Point out that "blared" suggests the sound of a smoke detector and adds vigor to the scene.

    The magician smiled as the green powder *fizzed* in the potion.

    Note that "fizzed" relates the sound it describes.

3. Encourage students to use onomatopoeic words when appropriate in their writing.

Extension:

• Distribute copies of the accompanying "Onomatopoeic Words." Review the list of onomatopoeic words with your students. Students should try to add words to the list, and share their lists with partners or peer groups.

Onomatopoeic Words

Onomatopoeic words suggest the sounds they describe. They appeal to the sense of hearing. Bees buzz, cows moo, and lions roar. Following are several onomatopoeic words. After reviewing the list, work with a partner or peer group and see if you can add to it.

bang	hiss	sizzle
boom	honk	slurp
bow-wow	hoot	splash
clang	howl	squish
clink	hum	swish
coo	meow	tick-tock
crackle	moo	thud
cuckoo	neigh	thump
fizz	puff	tinkle
growl	rev	twang
grunt	ring	whiz

How many can you add?

_____

_____

_____

_____

MINI-LESSON 32:
USING ALLITERATION

Alliteration is the use of two or more words in a sentence that have the same beginning sounds. Effective use of alliteration can enhance writing style, add rhythm and flow to words, or emphasize ideas.

Procedure:

1. Explain what alliteration is.
2. Distribute copies of (or project) "A Sample of Alliteration," which highlights alliteration through poetry. Ask students to read the poem, then discuss the examples of alliteration:

    Line 1, "sun, sea" (note that "rises" also has an "s" sound which adds to the effect)

    Line 2, "glow, glare"

    Line 3, "burst, brightness"

    Line 4, "sweeps, sea" (note that "across" also has an "s" sound)

    Line 9, "brilliant, sunbeams" (although the "b" sound is on the second syllable, this still produces an alliterative sound)

    Line 11, "another, night"

    Line 12, "dominates, day"

3. Note that while these examples are of poetry, alliteration can also be used effectively in prose.
4. Caution students that while alliteration can add to their writing, too much of it can detract from their words and ideas.

Extension:

*   Ask students to work with a partner. Partners should read some of each other's previous writings and note examples of alliteration. They should then discuss how the alliteration enhanced the piece. They may also identify places where alliteration could be added to improve the piece.

A Sample of Alliteration

The following poem has several examples of alliteration. How many can you find?

Sunburst

1	The sun rises from the sea,
2	First a glow, then a glare.
3	Then a burst of brightness
4	That sweeps across the sea,
5	Making a dazzling golden road over
6	The waves to the land.
7	The morning star blazes,
8	But its light soon fades,
9	Scattered by brilliant sunbeams.
10	Only the moon waits in the west
11	For another night, its luster gone.
12	The sun dominates the new day.

MINI-LESSON 33:
CONFLICT

Conflict is an essential component of every story. It is the fuel for the plot. As characters try to solve the problems they encounter in a story, they inevitably find themselves in conflict with others, their environment, or themselves. (See Mini-lesson 11, "Writing Fiction," for information on plots.)

Procedure:

1. Explain that conflict is a vital part of every story. Without it, there would be no action, suspense, or urgency. Stories would be boring.

2. Explain conflict in terms of goals. Characters have goals — things that they want to achieve. As they try to reach their goals, they are blocked by others, by the environment, or by their own limitations. Trying to overcome those obstacles puts the characters in conflict.

3. Distribute copies of the outline for the story, "The Runaway." Review it with your students and discuss the conflict that arises out of the plot.

   a. In the opening the conflict arises between Sue and her mother over Eddie.

   b. After Sue runs away, she is in conflict with Eddie, who tries to convince her to go home.

   c. At the bus stop, Sue is in conflict with herself as she struggles to decide what to do.

   d. The resolution of the story occurs when she decides to go home and try to solve the problem.

Extensions:

- Suggest that students look for conflict in stories they read and see how it arises from the plot.

- Conduct a class discussion about the conflict in a story students have read or a movie they have watched.

The Runaway

Read the following plot outline of the story, and decide what the conflict is. Notice how the conflict switches between people.

I. Opening — Sue walks home from school with Eddie, her boyfriend. They stop a few blocks from her house. Sue is not supposed to be seeing Eddie because her parents disapprove of him. They say he is not good enough for her. Unknown to Sue and Eddie, her mother is driving by and sees her with Eddie.

II. Sue arrives home. Her mother is waiting for her and they argue about Eddie. Sue believes that her parents do not understand her; her mother counters that Sue is too young to understand what is good for her. Crying, Sue runs to her room.

III. Later that night, Sue decides to run away. She packs some things and slips out. She goes to Eddie's house. When she tells him what she's doing, he tries to convince her that what she is doing won't solve the problem. Sue refuses to listen to him and runs off before he can stop her.

IV. Eddie calls Sue's parents and tells them what has happened. At first her parents don't believe him, but when Sue's mother checks her room, she realizes that Eddie is telling the truth. Together, Eddie and Sue's parents begin searching for her.

V. It is late at night. Sue is waiting, alone, at a bus stop. She is thinking about what Eddie said that running won't solve their problem. She also thinks about her feelings for him, and her love for her parents. She begins to realize that he was right. Finally, she decides to go home. She meets Eddie and her parents at the front door of the bus stop.

MINI-LESSON 34: CHARACTERIZATION

Characterization is the way a writer delineates her characters. Effective characterization is achieved by revealing the natures of characters and making them seem like real people with whom readers can identify.

Procedure:

1. Mention that when we think of a good story, we usually think of the characters. It is hard to think of a story without recalling the characters.

2. Explain that authors invent characters and show their traits through actions, descriptions, dialogue, and thoughts. In this way they reveal the natures of characters.

3. Distribute copies of the accompanying "Revealing Character" and review the sheet with your students. Identify the different traits the examples show.

    Through Action:

    Example 1: Joe is dishonest.
    Example 2: Jan is courageous.
    Example 3: Julio is confident.
    Example 4: Peter is unconfident.
    Example 5: Alice is trustworthy.

    Through Description:
    Example 6: Samantha's hair is brown and curly.
    Example 7: Mario is big and strong for a fourteen-year-old boy.
    Example 8: Bailey is mean.

    Through Thoughts:
    Example 9: Marty gives up easily.
    Example 10: Marsha is determined.

4. Caution students not to overcharacterize. Readers don't need to know every detail about a character. They don't need to know everything a character wears or witness every thought. Only those traits that are necessary to the story should be revealed. Minor characters may need only one or two traits.

5. Emphasize that the actions of characters must always be motivated. They must have a logical reason for doing the things they do.

6. Note that names should fit the personalities of characters. Names carry impressions. Laurie, for instance, sounds like a wholesome young woman. Hacker sounds like a tough guy — a good name for a detective. Sydney sounds bookish or nerdy, but Sid doesn't.

7. Mention that character tags refer to favorite phrases, gestures, or mannerisms like snapping the fingers or clicking the tongue that a character does repeatedly. Tags are excellent ways to characterize because they reinforce an impression on readers, but they must be used with care so that they don't become tiresome.

Extensions:

- Ask students to think of a favorite character from a story, TV show, or movie. Distribute copies of the "Character Chart" and ask them to identify that character's traits. They should share their charts with a partner or peer groups.

- Distribute copies of the "Character Chart" for students to use in the creation of characters for their own stories. Explain that many professional authors use character charts to help them develop characters. Mention that there are many types of charts and that this is a common example.

- Suggest that students focus their attention on characterization as they read a story or watch a movie or TV show. They should ask themselves the following:

  How are characters developed?

  What traits are revealed?

  How are the traits revealed?

Revealing Character

You can reveal your characters to readers in three ways:

Through Action:

- What the character does.

    Example 1: Joe steals a bike.

    Example 2: The building is on fire, and Jan rushes in and saves her little sister.

- What the character says.

    Example 3: "I think we can do it," Julio said, looking up at the mountain.

    Example 4: "We'll never make it," Peter said, looking up at the mountain.

- What other characters say or think about a character.

    Example 5: "Alice Foster is one person you can count on," Jake said.

Through Description

Example 6: Samantha's brown hair curled down to her shoulders.

Example 7: Mario's muscles bulged as he helped his father move the couch. At fourteen he was big for his age and could lift as much as many men.

Example 8: Bailey's eyes were cold and blue and he talked like the bad guy in a typical Western — slowly, between gritted teeth, as if he might lose his patience at any moment and just shoot you.

Through Thoughts

Example 9: I'll never pass that test, Marty thought, sighing. It's hopeless.

Example 10: Marsha thought of the upcoming swim meet. There's no way I'll let Deanna beat me.

Character Chart

CHARACTER'S NAME _____ Age _____

Background _____

_____

Positive traits _____

_____

_____

Negative traits _____

_____

_____

Ambitions/goals _____

_____

_____

Clothing _____

_____

Most distinctive trait _____

Color eyes _____ Glasses/contacts _____

Color hair _____ Hair style _____

Height _____ Weight _____

What other people think of the character _____

_____

_____

_____

MINI-LESSON 35: WRITING DIALOGUE

Dialogue is an important element of any story. It adds to the action and allows readers to listen to what the characters say. Characters become credible through effective dialogue. Without characters conversing, most stories would be flat and uninteresting.

Procedure:

1. Explain that dialogue occurs when characters speak to each other.

2. Point out that dialogue is an important part of any story. It is a major part of action and can help to show conflicts, thoughts, motivations, and goals. It should always be a part of the plot and move the story forward.

3. Explain that characters should seem to sound the way people really speak. For example, most people speak in short sentences and phrases. Most use contractions. The words of characters should match the setting of a story and their life-style. For example, people of sixteenth-century England speak differently than people today. A rich woman will talk differently from someone who has known poverty all his life. However, dialogue in stories can't be exactly the same as in real life — the "Uhs," "Ahs," and "You knows" would be too distracting. (And some real-life dialogue is inappropriate for school writing.)

4. Distribute copies of "Dialogue Samples." Review the examples on the sheet and point out the correct way to write dialogue. Especially note that in Example 2, a comma follows said and the "a" in "at" is lower case. In Example 3, a period follows Joe, and the "T" in "Those" is capitalized. In Example 4, the question mark takes the place of a comma.

5. Suggest that students look at an example of published dialogue in a story or book when they need to refresh their memory of the rules of punctuation for dialogue.

Extension:

- Suggest that students study the dialogue of characters in stories they read and ask themselves the following questions:

   Why do the character's words sound realistic?

   How do the words show what kind of person the character is?

Dialogue Samples

Dialogue is an important part of most stories. When writing dialogue, remember:

- Dialogue requires the use of quotation marks.
- Commas and end marks always go inside the quotation marks.
- The words of new speakers begin new paragraphs.
- Dialogue should always be a part of the plot and move the story forward.

Study these examples:

1. "It looks like rain today," said Joe. He pointed at the dark clouds. "I bet our baseball game will be rained out."

2. "The rain might hold off," Mary Ellen said, "at least until the game is done."

3. "I doubt it," said Joe. "Those clouds are going to open up any minute."

4. "Do you really think so?" asked Mary Ellen. "It seems a little brighter back toward town."

MINI-LESSON 36: DEVELOPING SETTINGS

The setting of a story is the background against which a story takes place. The setting can be an open prairie, a residential neighborhood, or the inside of a spaceship. The setting of a story is important because it helps to build and shape mood.

Procedure:

1. Explain that the setting of a story is the time and place a story happens.

2. Note that the setting helps to build and shape mood. For example, a dark, cold rainy night in an old castle provides a good setting for a ghost story or a murder mystery. The setting should always support the action of a story.

3. Explain that the best way to describe settings is by weaving descriptions in with the action. In this way the action keeps moving. When too much description is given in a paragraph, readers often skip over it so that they can continue with the action. By weaving description in with action, details of the setting are given and the action keeps moving.

4. Hand out copies of the accompanying "Setting Samples." Instruct students to read the two examples in which the setting is described.

   a. Point out that although the first offers good details, it slows the action.

   b. In the second example, the setting is interwoven with the action, keeping the story moving forward.

Extension:

- Suggest that students take a story they wrote earlier and look for places where they might have written too much description. They should revise the story and interweave the description of the setting with the action.

Setting Samples

Following are two examples of how to write settings. In Sample 1, the setting is described in one paragraph. In Sample 2, it is woven through the action. Which one do you like?

Sample 1

Tom looked at Jason.

"This can't be the place," Tom said nervously.

The dark house loomed before them, brightened eerily by the glow of the full moon. A broken sign, confirming the address, hung crookedly on the front of the rusty iron fence that surrounded the weed-choked property. The place looked to be 200 years old. A gust of wind blew one of the shutters, making it creak.

"Sam said to meet him here," Jason said.

"You sure you want to join this club?" said Tom.

"If we want to be paranormal investigators, I suppose this is a good place to start," said Jason. He forced a smile. "Let's go inside . . ."

Sample 2

Tom looked at Jason.

"This can't be the place," Tom said nervously. The dark house loomed before them, brightened eerily by the glow of the full moon.

"Sam said to meet him here," Jason said. "That's the address." He pointed at the broken sign on the rusty iron fence that surrounded the weed-choked property.

Tom swallowed hard. "You sure you want to join this club?" He looked at the house again. "That place must be 200 years old." He shuddered as a gust of wind blew one of the shutters and made it creak.

"If we want to be paranormal investigators, I suppose this is a good place to start," said Jason. He forced a smile. "Let's go inside . . ."

MINI-LESSON 37:
USING FLASHBACKS

Flashbacks are an author's device through which current action can be explained by events and action that happened in the past. A character's current fear of heights, for example, can easily be shown through a flashback.

Procedure:

1. Tell students that authors use flashbacks to explain current action that is a result of past events. Flashbacks are used when providing that past information with the current action would disrupt the story. Here's an example: a sixteen-year-old girl is afraid of dogs because she was attacked by a dog when she was five. To open the story when the girl is five just to show why she is afraid of dogs would be impractical. Instead, the author uses a flashback.

2. Distribute copies of the accompanying sample story, "The Party." Allow students a few minutes to read the story; then ask them to point out the flashback — Monica's recalling the party at her previous town and the tragedy that resulted. Explain that the flashback is necessary for the reader to understand Monica's action of leaving the party. Note how the flashback is entered smoothly and how the last sentence of the flashback leads back into the current action.

3. Warn students to use flashbacks carefully. Unnecessary flashbacks slow the action and confuse or frustrate readers. Flashbacks should be used only when a past event affects the current action.

Extension:

- Suggest that students look for examples of flashbacks in stories they read. They should share their findings with the class, a partner, or their peer groups, explaining how the flashback is necessary to the story.

The Party

Monica was excited as she and Lisa hurried up the front steps to Deena's house. This was the first party she had been invited to since she had moved to Glennville three months ago. At first she had had trouble making friends, but now she felt that she was a friend of one of the most popular girls in school — Deena Sanford.

"This is going to be a great party," Lisa said as she rang the doorbell. "Deena's parents aren't home."

The way she said that bothered Monica. "They're not?"

"No. Isn't that fantastic?"

Before Monica could answer, Deena opened the door and greeted them. Several kids were already there. Music blared from a stereo and kids were dancing. It was a lot louder and wilder than Monica thought it would be.

She mingled with the other kids, who seemed glad that she had come. That made Monica feel accepted.

Just as Monica was starting to relax, Deena emerged from the kitchen with several cans of beer on a tray.

"Here's what everybody's been waiting for," she announced.

Monica watched as her friends crowded around Deena, eager for a can of beer. Monica's mind flew back to this same scene in her former town. There was drinking at that party, too. She recalled how she and her best friend, Stacy, had become drunk, and then, walking home, Stacy had been hit by a car. Remembering the flashing lights, the sirens, the questions, and explanations made her shudder. That Stacy had recovered made little difference to Monica now.

When Deena handed Monica a can, Monica shook her head.

"Oh come on," said Deena. "Take one. You won't get into any trouble."

"No," Monica said. "I don't want any." She headed to the closet to get her coat. Pulling her coat on, she left.

MINI-LESSON 38:
Foreshadowing

An author uses foreshadowing to hint at events to come and arouse anticipation in the reader. Foreshadowing makes action believable because the reader can see a logical progression of events. Foreshadowing is used in virtually all types of fiction.

Procedure:

1. Explain that foreshadowing is an author's device that hints of events to come in a story. Use this example:

    The author mentions that dark clouds are gathering in the western sky. Later, a tornado hits the town.

    This event is believable because it was foreshadowed.

2. Mention that foreshadowing should be done subtly. It works best when it is interwoven with the action. Foreshadowing should always be an outgrowth of the plot and not call attention to itself.

3. Distribute copies of "Foreshadowing Sample." Allow your students time to read the material, then point out the examples of foreshadowing:

    Paragraph 1 — the heat and humidity

    Paragraph 3 — the skittish horse

    Paragraph 6 — the high thunderheads looming

    Paragraph 7 — the increasing wind and the dark clouds stretched over the land

    All these foreshadow the storm. Without them the storm would simply appear and the story would lose believability.

Extension:

- Ask students to look for examples of foreshadowing in stories they read. They should share examples with partners or peer groups and discuss how the author used foreshadowing.

Foreshadowing Sample

Sweat beaded Brad's forehead and his shirt stuck to his back as he helped his father feed the horses in the corral. Even though it was early morning, the humidity was like the kind that came late in the afternoon.

After feeding the horses, Brad's father went to buy supplies, and Brad started repairing the rails on the corral behind the barn. He enjoyed working with his hands and, within an hour, had the broken rails replaced. Standing back, he smiled. He looked forward to the school year ending so that he could help his father on the ranch every day. During school he only worked on Saturdays.

As he stood back and admired his work, he noticed that the horses seemed skittish. Walking to the corral, Brad tried calming them by speaking with a soothing voice. He had never seen them like this.

He watched his father drive up in the pickup truck filled with supplies he had gotten in town.

"Give me a hand unloading," his father said. "I don't like the looks of that." He nodded toward the west.

Brad turned and saw the high thunderheads looming like angry giants in the distance. "We'd better hurry," he said.

By the time they finished unloading the supplies the wind had started blowing and dark clouds filled the sky.

"This'll be a big one," Brad said as the first raindrops began to fall.

His father's voice was sharp. "Go inside and take your mother down to the basement."

Brad turned and looked in the direction of his father's gaze. A huge funnel cloud was dropping out of the sky.

"Hurry!" his father said.

Brad ran for the back door, his heart pounding.

"Mom! Mom! Tornado!"

MINI-LESSON 39:
THE CLIMAX

The climax of a story is that moment when the lead character either solves his problem or he fails. It is distinct from the ending of the story, which serves to tie any loose ends together.

Procedure:

1. Explain that the climax is the point of the story where the lead character either succeeds or fails to solve his problem.

2. Explain that for a climax to be satisfactory, it must grow logically out of the plot. Problems can't be solved through coincidence or luck. Good climaxes result when the lead character solves the problem himself. He can't do something that is out of his powers.

3. Note that the ending of a story follows the climax. The ending shows the aftermath of the climax.

4. Share these climaxes that should be avoided because they are weak or clichéd.

   The lead character faces incredible hardship. When everything seems hopeless, he wakes up. It was only a dream.

   The lead wakes up from the dream, only to find that the dream is coming true.

   When failure seems inevitable, a rich uncle, aunt, or lost parent arrives to save the day.

   The problem turns out to be a misunderstanding. There was never a real problem.

   The character performs an amazing feat of supernatural strength.

   The character is saved by luck or coincidence.

Extension:

- Talk about the climaxes in some recent stories or movies.

MINI-LESSON 40:
PLAGIARISM

Plagiarism occurs when a writer takes the words or expressions of another author and claims them explicitly or implicitly (through failure to use proper credits) as his or her own. Plagiarism is stealing and is a violation of copyright laws.

Procedure:

1. Explain that plagiarism violates copyright laws. Copyright laws insure that an author's work remains hers and prevents others from copying it without receiving permission.

2. Emphasize that plagiarism is unethical. Students can make "fair use" of published material, but they must credit the author properly. Plagiarism is not only stealing, but cheating.

3. Distribute copies of (or project) the accompanying "Footnoting" and review it with your students.

Footnoting

To avoid plagiarism, you must give proper credit to the authors from whom you borrow material. You provide credit with footnotes. You should credit direct quotes, specific ideas used by another writer, an opinion of another, and any displays such as tables, charts, or diagrams that have been used in other works.

To credit information, authors identify the source. Quoted material can be linked to its source either through an asterisk or numbers. Footnotes often appear at the bottom or "foot" of the page. When they appear at the end of a chapter, or at the end of a report or book, they are called "endnotes."

There are many formats for notes. Following are some examples:

Book, one author

Carl Sagan, *Cosmos*, p. 129.

Book, two or three authors

Gerard I. Nierenberg and Henry H. Calero, *How to Read a Person Like a Book*, p. 65.

Book, more than three authors

Robert E. Eicholz et al., *Addison-Wesley Mathematics, Book 6*, p. 222.

A magazine or newspaper article

Lawrence E. Joseph, "The Scoop on Ice Cream," *Discover* (August 1992), p. 69.

MINI-LESSON 41:
CHOOSING TITLES

Few students spend much time selecting titles for their pieces. The title, however, is the initial hook that catches a reader's attention. Moreover, a good title can lead smoothly into the piece.

Procedure:

1. Explain that titles are important to every piece. Good titles capture the attention of readers and lead them into the opening of the piece.

2. Distribute copies of "Titles" and review the information about titles with your students.

3. Emphasize that titles should always fit the piece that follows.

Extension:

• Suggest that students work with a partner and brainstorm titles. The first student gives one of her stories, articles, or poems to her partner. After the partner reads the piece, together the students brainstorm possible titles. They should write down every title that comes to mind. (Give them a minimum number or very few may come to mind!) After brainstorming, the author selects the title for the piece. The second student now gives one of his stories, articles, or poems to his partner to read. They then brainstorm possible titles for this piece. After brainstorming, the author selects the title. This activity permits students to see a variety of potential titles for their work.

Titles

For *nonfiction*, titles should be appealing and informative. Following are examples of possible titles for some common types of nonfiction.

- General nonfiction titles usually refer to the focus of the piece, taking into account the slant. Here are some examples:

    A piece about homework may be titled
    "Homework Blues," "A Waste of Time," "The Burden of Youth," or "How Much Homework Is Too Much?"

    A piece on places to take a date may be titled
    "Great Places for Dates!" "Romantic and Inexpensive," or "The 'In' Places."

- Titles for how-to pieces tell the reader exactly what the article will tell him. Here are some examples:

    "How to Build a Backyard Bird Feeder"
    "10 Easy Steps to Financial Success"
    "Homework Without Tears"
    "How to Get Straight A's Without Trying"

- Articles for essays or persuasive pieces usually focus on the topic:

    "Should Girls Play on Boys' Teams?"
    "It's Time for an Open Lunch for Seniors"
    "The Case Against the Incinerator"

For *fiction*, titles may describe the story or may highlight a key part of the plot. Sometimes the title may refer to an idea central to the story's theme. Following are some examples:

    A story in which everything goes wrong for the lead character
    — "Harry's Tough Night"

    A story about an unusual family that comes to live in a small town — "The Family"

    A story about a girl who suffers from depression — "Zero"

[handwritten margin notes:] gives a "feeling" · information · question · general theme

Mini-lessons for the Mechanics of Writing

MINI-LESSON 42:
WHAT IS GRAMMAR?

Grammar refers to the system of rules in language by which sentences are constructed. A superior understanding of grammar doesn't ensure that a student will be able to write well, but an inferior understanding automatically condemns a student to poor writing.

Procedure:

1. Explain that grammar refers to the rules and customs of English that govern the way sentences are constructed. Without grammatical rules, everyone would write and speak as he or she wished, making communication confusing, if not, at times, impossible. Ask students to imagine driving along a highway where motorists followed their own driving rules. Ask them what would likely happen. Just as driving laws and customs ensure an orderly passage of traffic on our roadways (in most cases, at least!), grammar helps ensure that we communicate through language in a way that others can understand.

2. Emphasize that understanding grammar can help authors express themselves clearly. Understanding grammar enables a writer to clarify the meaning of his or her sentences for the reader's benefit. On the board or an overhead projector, offer the following examples. Note how the changes in punctuation changed the meanings of the sentences. This is what grammar is all about.

   The teacher stood at the front of the room and called the students' names.
   The teacher stood at the front of the room and called the students names.

   Miss Morales, the supervisor, inspected the finished products.
   Miss Morales, the supervisor inspected the finished products.

   Seth said, "I like to clown around."
   Seth said I like to clown around.

MINI-LESSON 43:
SUBJECT-VERB AGREEMENT

Subjects must always agree with their verbs. While this is not usually a problem for your good writers, many students will benefit from a review on this topic.

Procedure:

1. Explain that singular subjects require the singular form of verbs and that plural subjects require the plural forms of verbs. Subjects and verbs must always agree in number.

2. Using the board or an overhead projector, offer these examples of singular subjects and verbs in the present tense:

   Juan works at the supermarket after school.
   He rides his bike to school.

   Note that each subject represents one and takes the singular form of the verb.

3. Offer these examples of plural subjects —

   The boys work at the supermarket after school.
   They ride their bikes to school.

   Note the plural forms of the verbs.

4. Mention that "I" and "you" take the plural form of verbs in the present tense. Offer these examples:

   I work at the supermarket after school.
   You ride your bike to school.

5. Note that the past tenses of verbs, except the verb "to be," is the same for singular and plural subjects. Offer these examples:

   Juan worked at the supermarket after school.
   The boys worked at the supermarket after school.

   The boy rode his bike to school.
   The boys rode their bikes to school.

MINI-LESSON 44:
COMPOUND SUBJECT-VERB AGREEMENT

A compound subject is formed when two words or groups of words are connected to form the subject of a verb. This causes agreement confusion for some students.

Procedure:

1. Explain that a verb may have compound subjects — two words or groups of words that form the subject. Depending on how they are connected, compound subjects may take either singular or plural verbs.

2. Explain that when subjects are joined by *and* they require a plural verb. Offer these examples on the board or an overhead projector:

   Victor and Serge look like brothers.
   The puppy and kitten play together constantly.

3. Explain that when subjects are joined by *or* or *nor* they take a singular verb. Offer these examples:

   Either Ali or Bert collects tickets at the front door.
   Neither Reg nor Maria has the directions to the party.

MINI-LESSON 45:
SUBJECT-VERB AGREEMENT WITH INTERVENING PHRASES_____

While most students have little trouble with the agreement between subjects and verbs when the verb directly follows the subject, sentences where phrases come between the subject and verb can pose problems.

Procedure:

1. Remind students that subjects and verbs must always agree in number. While in most cases this is relatively easy to do, some sentences require the careful attention of the writer to make sure that her subjects and verbs agree.

2. Write this sentence on the board or an overhead projector:

    The winner, along with the other finalists, receives her award tonight.

    Ask students to identify the subject and verb of the sentence. Some will say "finalists" is the subject and "receives" is the verb. "Receives" is the verb, of course, but "winner" is the subject. In its simplest form the sentence is

    The winner receives her award tonight.

    Emphasize that this is a common agreement mistake. When a person writes a sentence in which the subject and verb are separated, the mind often links the verb with the nearest noun. Even professional authors make this mistake.

3. Offer these additional examples and point out the subjects and verbs:

    The manager, as well as the fans, was angry at the umpire's call.

    The number of compulsory figures was the same for all contestants.

    Tamara, with three other students, writes the school announcements each morning.

MINI-LESSON 46:
SUBJECT-VERB AGREEMENT — DOESN'T OR DON'T_____

A common agreement mistake students make is using "don't" with a singular subject, as in "He don't go any more."

Procedure:

1. Explain that the contractions "doesn't" and "don't" often lead to mistakes in agreement.

2. Note that "not" is not a part of the verb. To ensure correct agreement of subjects with "doesn't" and "don't," authors much match the subject of the sentence with "does" or "do." Offer these examples on the board or an overhead projector:

   singular subject
      He doesn't finish his homework at night.
      He does not finish his homework at night.

   plural subject
      They don't finish their homework at night.
      They do not finish their homework at night.

3. Emphasize these nonstandard sentences:

      He don't like history.
      She don't believe in magic.

   Ask how to correct them. Obvious suggestions would be the following:

      He doesn't like history.
      She doesn't believe in magic.

4. Suggest that to be sure they are using the correct forms, students should break the contraction into two words and see if the subjects and verbs agree. Offer this example:

      She don't want to go skating.
      She do not want to go skating.

   Breaking the contractions often helps students to see problems with agreement.

MINI-LESSON 47:
SUBJECT-VERB AGREEMENT — THERE'S AND HERE'S

In conversation we may say something like, "There's two ways you can go." Because students often write the way they speak, those types of constructions may slip into their writing. Although they may be acceptable in conversation, they highlight an agreement problem in written language.

Procedure:

1. Emphasize that subject-verb agreement is important to written English. Offer these two sentences on the board or an overhead projector:

    There's two ways you can go.
    There're two ways you can go.

    Ask students, by a show of hands, who thinks the first sentence is correct. Then the second.

2. Explain that the second is correct because "ways" is the subject of the sentence and it requires "are" for its verb. Without the contraction the sentence would read:

    There are two ways to go.

3. Suggest that students break down contractions to make sure that they don't use constructions with faulty agreement. Offer these examples:

    Where's your sisters?
    Where is your sisters?
    This should be "Where are . . ."

    Here's your boots, scarf, and gloves.
    Here is your boots, scarf, and gloves.
    This should be "Here are . . ."

MINI-LESSON 48:
SUBJECT-VERB AGREEMENT — INDEFINITE PRONOUNS

Indefinite pronouns often cause agreement problems because they don't point to a specific subject.

Procedure:

1. Explain that indefinite pronouns are words that do not refer to a specific person, place, or thing. When used as subjects, they must agree with verbs.

2. Explain that some indefinite pronouns are always singular and take the singular form of verbs. Offer these examples on the board or an overhead projector:

    each, either, neither, anyone, anybody, anything, something, someone, somebody, everyone, one, everything, everybody, nothing, no one, none

    Offer these sentences:

    Everybody wants to be successful.
    Each of the girls has her ticket.

3. Explain that some indefinite pronouns are always plural and take the plural form of verbs:

    few, many, several, both, others

    Offer these sentences:

    Both of the schedules have mistakes.
    Few were correct.

4. Note that some indefinite pronouns can be singular or plural, depending on how they are used in the sentence.

    all, any, some, most, none

    Offer these sentences —

    Some of the problems were correct. (*plural*)
    Some of the problem was correct. (*singular*)

MINI-LESSON 49: SUBJECT (PRONOUN)-VERB AGREEMENT

Most of the pronoun forms present few problems for your students because the pronouns are used in written language the same way they are used in conversation. A few, however, especially when used as the subjects of sentences, are often used incorrectly in conversation or speech. It's little wonder they are often used incorrectly in written language, too.

Procedure:

1. On the board or an overhead projector list the subject pronouns:

   I, you, he, she, it, we, they, who, whoever

   Emphasize that only these can be used as the subjects of sentences.

2. Mention that some pronouns consistently are used incorrectly as subjects. Offer these examples:

   Example 1
   Her and I play tennis together. ("Her" should be "She.")

   Example 2
   Tom and me are going swimming after school. ("Me" should be "I.")

3. Explain that a good test to be sure that they have used subject pronouns correctly in sentences like the examples is to separate the pronouns and read each with the verb. Offer these examples:

   In Example 1, reread it like this:
   I play tennis. (This is good.)
   Her play tennis. (This is clearly wrong.)

   In Example 2, reread it like this:
   Tom is going swimming. (This sounds fine.)
   Me is going swimming. (Obviously wrong.)

MINI-LESSON 50:
AGREEMENT OF PRONOUNS AND ANTECEDENTS_____

Many of the agreement problems your students will have are likely to center on subjects and verbs. Some students, however, will have problems with the agreement between pronouns and antecedents and will benefit from a mini-lesson on the topic.

Procedure:

1. Explain that the antecedent of a pronoun is the word in a sentence to which the pronoun refers. If the antecedent is singular, the pronoun must be singular. If the antecedent is plural, the pronoun must be plural. If the antecedent is masculine, for example, the pronoun must be masculine. Offer these examples on the board or an overhead projector:

   Manuel twisted *his* ankle at baseball practice.

   Note that Manuel is singular and agrees with "his."

   Debbie and Rose argued *their* points well.

   Debbie and Rose are plural and agree with "their."

2. Explain that singular indefinite pronouns should be linked with singular pronouns. Offer this example of a common mistake:

   Everybody put *their* coats on.

   Explain that although this construction is used in conversations every day, it is technically incorrect. "Everybody" is singular and requires singular pronouns. "Their" is plural.

   Offer ways this sentence can be corrected:

   Everybody put *his or her* coat on.
   Everybody put *his* coat on.
   Everybody put *her* coat on.
   They all put *their* coats on.

   Mention that the trend today is to be nonsexist. If using the phrase "his or her" proves to be awkward, authors often alternate the use of "his" and "her." Whenever possible, many authors use a plural construction.

MINI-LESSON 51:
POSSESSIVE NOUNS

The possessive case of nouns gives many students (and their teachers) severe headaches. While most students readily grasp the concept of ownership, using apostrophes correctly to denote that ownership in their writing often turns out to be guesswork. Even when they get the apostrophes right, some students don't know why.

Procedure:

1. Explain that when a noun is used to show that a thing belongs to someone or something, an apostrophe is needed.

2. Emphasize that the possessive case of nouns is determined by three rules. Explain the rules and offer examples on the board or an overhead projector.

    a. The possessive case of singular nouns is formed by adding an apostrophe and an *s*.

        the dog's leash   Morris's keys
        New York's skyline   Janice's car

    Note that for words that have more than one syllable and which end in an *s*-sound, it is acceptable (but not required) to form the singular possessive by adding only the apostrophe. The purpose of this is to avoid too many *s*-sounds.

        Moses' Commandments   the princess' ring

    b. The possessive case of plural nouns that end in *s* is formed by adding an apostrophe.

        the two boys' camping equipment
        the puppies' pillow

    c. The possessive case of plural nouns that do not end in *s* is formed by adding an apostrophe *s*.

        the women's basketball team
        the children's playhouse

3. Emphasize that the possessive case of nouns always requires an apostrophe.

MINI-LESSON 52:
PARAGRAPHING

While most of your students will know that a paragraph is a group of related sentences about a main idea, many will have trouble developing solid paragraphs. A review of paragraphing can be helpful, or even necessary, for many students.

Procedure:

1. Explain that a paragraph is a group of sentences that describes a main idea. A paragraph is usually a part of a larger work, but it can be a unit in itself. This is especially true of short essays.

2. Explain that, in nonfiction, paragraphs usually have three parts:

   a. A *topic sentence* which states the main idea.

   b. *Supporting sentences* which provide details about the main idea.

   c. A *concluding sentence* which summarizes or restates the main idea.

3. Explain that, in fiction, paragraphs are dependent upon various factors, including characters, action, dialogue, and suspense.

4. Mention that paragraphs are usually indented five spaces. (On some word processors, this may vary a bit, but most are around five.)

5. Mention that paragraphs vary in length. Every paragraph should explain its main idea fully.

6. Note the two most common weaknesses of paragraphs.

   a. The topic sentence is unclear. To correct this, the topic sentence should focus on the main idea.

   b. Too few details support the main idea. To correct this, general statements should be replaced with specific ones that clearly support the main idea.

Extensions:

- Distribute copies of the accompanying "Developing Paragraphs, Sample 1." Instruct your students to read the selection about alligators. Point out that it lacks paragraphs and instruct them to mark where they feel new paragraphs should begin. When they are done, discuss where the paragraphs should be. You may distribute copies of (or project) the accompanying "Developing Paragraphs, Sample 2," which shows where new paragraphs should begin.

- Suggest that students reread a work in progress and look for examples of weak paragraphs. They should revise the paragraphs.

Developing Paragraphs, Sample 1

Read the following selection and mark where you think new paragraphs should start.

Return of the Alligator

A few hundred years ago, alligators thrived in the southeastern part of the United States. It is estimated that Florida alone had more than a million of these reptiles. With the coming of great numbers of people during the colonial period, the days of alligator supremacy were about to end. Alligators were hunted for sport and killed for their hide, which was made into prized leather. As farms, towns, and cities spread across the land, alligator habitats were destroyed. By the mid-1960s alligators were in danger of becoming extinct, and in 1967 they were declared an endangered species. Hunting was prohibited, and habitats were protected. It was hoped that such measures would enable the alligator population to increase. Alligators have taken advantage of this protection. They have made a remarkable comeback. Their numbers have grown so rapidly that some states again allow hunting. In fact, there are so many alligators in parts of Florida that they wander onto lawns and find their way into residential swimming pools!

Developing Paragraphs, Sample 2

Return of the Alligator

A few hundred years ago, alligators thrived in the southeastern part of the United States. It is estimated that Florida alone had more than a million of these reptiles.

With the coming of great numbers of people during the colonial period, the days of alligator supremacy were about to end. Alligators were hunted for sport and killed for their hide, which was made into prized leather. As farms, towns, and cities spread across the land, alligator habitats were destroyed.

By the mid-1960s alligators were in danger of becoming extinct, and in 1967 they were declared an endangered species. Hunting was prohibited, and habitats were protected. It was hoped that such measures would enable the alligator population to increase.

Alligators have taken advantage of this protection, and have made a remarkable comeback. Their numbers have grown so rapidly that some states again allow hunting. In fact, there are so many alligators in parts of Florida that they wander onto lawns and find their way into residential swimming pools!

MINI-LESSON 53:
VARYING SENTENCES TO MAKE WRITING INTERESTING_____

I often remind my students that a piece can be technically sound, yet not be an example of good, interesting writing. Such writing is often bland or monotonous, adding up to boring. In many cases, such pieces lack a variety of sentence constructions.

Procedure:

1. Explain that writing flows when the author uses a variety of sentence constructions and sentence lengths.

2. On the board or an overhead projector, offer these sentences with their revisions that demonstrate how sentence structure can be varied. Note how easily sentences can be varied by repositioning phrases and making minor changes to clauses.

> The storm clouds appeared without warning.
> Without warning, the storm clouds appeared.

> He soon became exhausted and had to drop out of the marathon.
> Soon becoming exhausted, he had to drop out of the marathon.

> Susan realized that she would not finish the report on time, because she couldn't obtain the research she needed.

> Because she couldn't obtain the research she needed, Susan realized that she would not finish the report on time.

Extension:

- Suggest that students reread a piece in progress and pay close attention to their sentence construction. They should revise where necessary to achieve variety in their constructions.

MINI-LESSON 54:
COMBINING SENTENCES FOR VARIATION_____

A major reason many students rely on simple sentences throughout entire pieces is because they are unsure how to construct longer sentences. To be safe, these students will use several simple sentences in succession, which makes writing choppy and awkward.

Procedure:

1. Remind students that varying sentences is necessary to make writing smooth.

2. Distribute copies of (or project) the accompanying "Why Combine Sentences?" Instruct students to read the two paragraphs and then discuss why the second one flows more smoothly than the first. Point out how combining some of the sentences enhanced the flow.

3. Emphasize that combining short sentences can vary sentence construction. Offer the following examples on the board or an overhead projector. Point out how the sentences were combined:

The human heart is a marvelous biological machine. It is the size of a person's closed fist.

The human heart, which is the size of a person's closed fist, is a marvelous biological machine.

Tanya had to do her homework. Then she went to work.

After Tanya did her homework, she went to work.

Saul came home at midnight. He was exhausted. He went right to sleep.

Exhausted, Saul came home at midnight and went right to sleep.

Ruby was sure that Tate had stolen Mrs. Wilson's purse. She didn't know what to do.

Ruby was sure that Tate had stolen Mrs. Wilson's purse, but she didn't know what to do.

Why Combine Sentences?

Read the following two paragraphs. Note how they are alike and how they are different. Which one flows more smoothly?

Randall looked in the mirror. He squirmed. He felt uncomfortable in the tux. He didn't like the way the jacket fit his shoulders. The collar was too tight. The bow tie seemed to be strangling him. He turned to see himself from different angles. He began to think that maybe it wasn't so bad. He was going to his sister's wedding. Plenty of her friends would be there. He should look his best.

Randall looked in the mirror and squirmed. He felt uncomfortable in the tux. He didn't like the way the jacket fit his shoulders, the collar was too tight, and the bow tie seemed to be strangling him. Turning to see himself from different angles, he began to think that maybe it wasn't so bad after all. He was going to his sister's wedding, and plenty of her friends would be there. He should look his best.

You probably realize that the first paragraph is monotonous and somewhat boring. Almost every sentence follows the same pattern. The second paragraph, however, combines many of the sentences, which helps the paragraph to flow more smoothly. This makes the writing more interesting.

MINI-LESSON 55:
SENTENCE FRAGMENTS

Fragments are incomplete sentences. Occasionally authors will use a fragment for emphasis or to enhance a mood, but in most cases fragments distract readers and should be avoided.

Procedure:

1. Explain that fragments are parts of sentences. They lack a subject or predicate (or both) and fail to express a complete thought. Offer these examples on the board or an overhead projector:

   The stars twinkled like diamonds. In the night sky.

   Point out that although "In the night sky" begins with a capital letter and ends with a period, it does not express a complete thought. It lacks a subject and predicate. Read by itself, it means nothing.

   Since he couldn't find his homework. Tom did it over.

   The opening clause is not a complete thought.

   Pam enjoys various activities. Such as skiing, horseback riding, and reading.

   The second statement lacks a subject and verb.

2. Explain that sometimes authors write fragments because they are writing as they are thinking. Since thoughts often come in short bursts, they may find their way into writing as sentence fragments.

3. Emphasize that the best way to avoid writing fragments is to make sure every sentence has a subject and predicate and expresses a complete thought.

4. Suggest that a good way to find fragments is to read each sentence out loud and see if it can stand alone. If it can't, it is a fragment.

5. Explain that the best way to correct fragments is to combine the fragment with another idea, making a new sentence. Fragments can also be corrected by adding the missing subject or verb.

Extensions:

- Students work with a partner and read a recent piece written by their partner. Each is to circle any fragments he or she finds in the partner's work. After discussing the fragments, authors should revise their work.

- Distribute copies of the accompanying "Find the Fragments." Instruct students to read the article, circle all the fragments, and revise them. Read the article and go over the revisions as a class.

  Answers: Because of fragments; parts of sentences that don't carry a complete thought; by reading your sentences out loud; to share your ideas. Accept any reasonable revisions.

Find the Fragments

Directions: Read the following piece and circle all the sentence fragments you find. Revise the fragments.

This piece is an example of poor writing. Because of fragments. Fragments are incomplete sentences. Parts of sentences that don't carry a full thought. Fragments make your writing rough and choppy. They call attention to themselves and steal the clarity of your ideas.

You can find fragments in your writing. By reading your sentences out loud. If a sentence can't stand alone, it is a fragment. You should revise it.

It's easy to revise fragments. You can combine the fragment with another idea and make a new sentence. Or you can add the missing subject or verb. Revising sentence fragments in your writing will make your writing smoother, and helps you. To share your ideas.

MINI-LESSON 56: RUN-ON SENTENCES

A run-on sentence is one that should be rewritten as two or more individual sentences. Instead of expressing one complete thought, or using a conjunction or semicolon to link two related thoughts, a run-on runs together more than one complete thought in a way that confuses or distracts most readers.

Procedure:

1. Explain that a run-on sentence is precisely what its name implies — it keeps going long after it should stop. A run-on sentence should be revised into two or more separate sentences. Offer these examples on the board or an overhead projector:

    (1) Peter is an excellent athlete, he lettered in three sports.

    Note that the comma after "athlete" should be a period. (A semicolon would also work.)

    (2) They went to the park they had a picnic.

    Point out the two separate thoughts in the sentence.

2. Explain that run-on sentences can be corrected in two ways. First, the run-on can be divided into two sentences, as Example 1 shows:

    Peter is an excellent athlete. He lettered in three sports.

    The second way is to revise the run-on with a conjunction, as Example 2 shows:

    They went to the park and they had a picnic.

3. Suggest that reading sentences out loud to see if each part of the sentence can stand alone is a good way to find run-on sentences. If the parts of a sentence can stand alone, it is likely to be a run-on. Also, suggest that students listen for pauses as they read aloud. A pause often indicates the need for a period.

MINI-LESSON 57:
*THE FIRST-PERSON POINT OF VIEW (POV)*_____

Many students find it difficult to maintain a consistent POV. (You'll undoubtedly have some in your workshop who have no idea of what point of view is.) They may start a piece in the first person, then switch to the third, or even the second, disrupting the unity of the piece. Since the first-person POV is one that almost all students use, I suggest that you start with it.

Procedure:

1. Explain that POV is the way an author tells his piece, whether it is fiction or nonfiction. Suggest that to gain an understanding of the first-person POV students imagine a camera resting on the shoulder of the lead character in a story. Whatever the camera records, the reader experiences. Things outside the camera's view are outside the POV, and the reader is not made aware of them. (The example of the camera also works well with the third-person limited POV. See Mini-lesson 58.)

2. Mention that there are many types of POVs; one of the easiest to use is the first-person POV. Personal narratives and autobiographies are examples of the first-person POV.

3. Explain that, in fiction, the first-person POV is a character, usually the lead, who tells the story as he or she participates in events. The viewpoint character refers to himself or herself as "I" throughout the story.

4. Distribute copies of (or project) the accompanying "First-Person POV Fact Sheet" and briefly review the information with your students.

5. Emphasize that once an author selects a POV, he or she should remain consistent with it and not switch to others.

Extension:

- Suggest that students find examples of the first-person POV in stories, articles, and books that they read. Tell them to note how the author remained consistent with the POV.

First-Person POV Fact Sheet

Advantages of the First-Person POV

1. The first-person POV makes it easy for an author to use his or her own voice. (However, this applies only in nonfiction or autobiographical fiction.)
2. It can be easier to write with power and emotion. After all, the narrator is a part, or an observer, of all the action.
3. It is often easier for authors to handle the emotions and thoughts of the viewpoint character, because the author assumes that character's role.

Disadvantages of the First-Person POV

1. The author can reveal only what the viewpoint character experiences or has learned about. For example, the narrator can't reveal the thoughts of other characters, unless he or she is a mind-reader.
2. The dramatic structure of the piece is limited to what the narrator participates in or learns about and can relate.

The following is an example of the first-person viewpoint.

I knew it was going to be a bad day when I stepped out of bed and stubbed my toe on the dresser. From there it only got worse. There was no hot water in the shower, I burnt my toast for breakfast, and found that a tire on my car had gone flat during the night.

When I arrived at work an hour late, my boss was waiting for me.

"Where have you been?" he said anxiously. "Mr. Hawkins has been here for a half-hour. You have the report for him, right?"

I groaned. The report was in the ledger — the one I had left on the kitchen table.

MINI-LESSON 58:
*THE THIRD-PERSON POINT OF VIEW (POV)*_____

The third-person POV is the most commonly used POV. It is sometimes called the "he/she" POV.

Procedure:

1. Explain that in the third-person POV the author takes a position outside the piece. The characters are referred to by name or as "he" or "she." The author is not a part of the action.

2. Explain that in the third-person POV, the author chooses the characters whose point-of-view he or she will use to tell the story. Tell your students to imagine a camera resting on each viewpoint character's shoulder recording the action. The reader experiences what the viewpoint character does.

3. Explain that, as with any POV, consistency is important. Shifting POVs unnecessarily is distracting to readers.

4. Distribute copies of (or project) the accompanying "Third-Person POV Fact Sheet" and review the information with your students. (Note that the example is the same as the one for the first-person POV but has been rewritten in the third person.)

Extension:

- Explain that the second-person POV is rarely used in fiction. In the second-person POV the author uses "You," as if the reader is a part of the action. For example,

    You walk through the meadow. The wind feels cool against your face; the grass is soft beneath your feet.

  The second-person POV forces the reader to be a part of the action, but the constant use of "you" can feel artificial. After all, the reader is not really a participant in the story.

Third-Person POV Fact Sheet

Advantages of the Third-Person POV

1. The third-person POV enables the author to set himself or herself apart from the action, making it easier to control the events of the story.
2. The third-person POV enables the author to control characters more easily than does the first-person POV.
3. The third-person POV allows the author to choose either a limited or omniscient POV.

Disadvantage of the Third-Person POV

The third-person POV can be more difficult than the first-person POV for some writers to handle. These writers often need the "immediacy" that the first-person POV provides to write with emotion and power.

The following is an example of the third-person POV.

Eddie knew it was going to be a bad day when he stepped out of bed and stubbed his toe on the dresser. From there it only got worse. There was no hot water in the shower, he burnt his toast for breakfast, and found that a tire on his car had gone flat during the night.

When he arrived at work an hour late, Eddie's boss was waiting for him.

"Where have you been?" he said anxiously. "Mr. Hawkins has been here for a half-hour. You have the report for him, right?"

Eddie groaned. The report was in the ledger—the one he had left on the kitchen table.

MINI-LESSON 59:
*LIMITED POINT OF VIEW (POV)*_____

Along with the choices of either first- or third-person POVs, your students should be aware of the difference between limited and omniscient POVs. In this mini-lesson, focus on the limited POV.

Procedure:

1. Explain that in a limited POV the author "limits" thoughts and emotions to his or her viewpoint character. The "camera" is over the shoulder of the viewpoint character.

2. Explain that by limiting the POV to the lead character, the reader knows only what the lead character knows. The reader lives through the story as the character does, resulting in a feeling of immediacy.

3. Distribute copies of (or project) the accompanying "Limited POV." Ask students to read the example, and then briefly lead a class discussion about the story. Point out how the author tells the story through Jessie's eyes, sharing her thoughts and feelings with the readers.

Extension:

- Suggest that students look for examples of limited POV in stories they read. They should pay close attention to the author's use of the POV.

Limited POV

The following story is written in the third-person, limited POV.

Final Batter

From the on-deck circle Jessie looked out across the field to the filled stands. The home crowd was roaring. She glanced up at the scoreboard: seven to six with one out, a runner on first in the bottom of the ninth. Already her team, the Stars, had scored three runs this inning.

"Come on, Maria!" Jessie called. She prayed that Maria would hit a homer and end the game. Jessie didn't want to bat with the game on the line. Her stomach was knotted with tension. "You can do it, Maria!"

Jessie watched anxiously as the count went to three balls and two strikes. Maria waited at the plate. The pitch came and the home crowd groaned — strike three.

"OK, Jessie!" said Lisa, the Stars' coach. "Just meet the ball . . . a hit keeps the rally going."

Jessie walked to the plate, the pressure nearly choking her. She passed Maria, who was slowly returning to the dugout.

"Wait for her curve, Jess," Maria said. "Nobody can hit that fastball."

Jessie nodded, thankful for the tip. Stepping into the batter's box, she tapped the plate and lifted her bat. She took a deep breath to steady her nerves.

"Wait for the curve," she said to herself. "Wait for the curve . . ."

The first two pitches were fastballs that Jessie let go. They were so fast that Jessie knew she could never hit them. Another fastball and the count went to one ball and two strikes. Jessie's hands tightened on the bat as the pitcher began her wind-up.

The pitch was a curve. It hung just a little over the plate. Recognizing her chance, Jessie swung and the ball shot off the bat, sailing far over the left-field fence.

MINI-LESSON 60:
OMNISCIENT POINT OF VIEW (POV)_____

The omniscient POV allows authors great latitude in telling their stories, because the authors can use multiple viewpoint characters.

Procedure:

1. Explain that unlike the limited POV in which the author "limits" the point of view to a lead character, the omniscient POV permits the author to utilize several characters to tell the story. The author has the freedom to move from character to character as necessary to tell the story effectively.

2. Mention that many novelists use the omniscient POV—they rely on multiple POVs to tell their stories. The authors switch smoothly among several viewpoint characters, usually at the end of chapters or scenes. Sometimes they switch viewpoint characters within a scene if the action demands it.

3. Note that authors must be careful not to switch viewpoint characters abruptly, or they might confuse their readers.

4. Distribute copies of (or project) the accompanying "Omniscient POV." Ask students to read the story and discuss how the author used the omniscient POV. Emphasize how the author included Lisa's thoughts in a POV switch. (Note that this story was also used for "Limited POV"; however, it is rewritten using an omniscient POV.)

5. Emphasize that the major advantage of the omniscient POV is that it allows authors to tell complicated stories, using the perspectives of various characters.

Omniscient POV

The following story is written in the third-person, omniscient POV.

Final Batter

From the on-deck circle Jessie looked out across the field to the filled stands. The home crowd was roaring. She glanced up at the scoreboard: seven to six with one out, a runner on first in the bottom of the ninth. Already her team, the Stars, had scored three runs this inning.

"Come on, Maria!" Jessie called. She prayed that Maria would hit a homer and end the game. Jessie didn't want to bat with the game on the line. Her stomach was knotted with tension. "You can do it, Maria!"

Jessie watched anxiously as the count went to three balls and two strikes. Maria waited at the plate. The pitch came and the home crowd groaned — strike three.

"OK, Jessie!" said Lisa, the Stars' coach. Lisa was worried. She knew that Jessie was no match for the girl who was pitching. "Just meet the ball . . . a hit keeps the rally going."

Jessie walked to the plate, the pressure nearly choking her. She passed Maria, who was slowly returning to the dugout.

"Wait for her curve, Jess," Maria said. "Nobody can hit that fastball."

Jessie nodded, thankful for the tip. Stepping into the batter's box, she tapped the plate and lifted her bat. She took a deep breath to steady her nerves.

"Wait for the curve," she said to herself. "Wait for the curve . . ."

The first two pitches were fastballs that Jessie let go. They were so fast that Jessie knew she could never hit them. Another fastball and the count went to one ball and two strikes. Jessie's hands tightened on the bat as the pitcher began her wind-up.

The pitch was a curve. It hung just a little over the plate. Recognizing her chance, Jessie swung and the ball shot off the bat, sailing far over the left-field fence.

MINI-LESSON 61:
AVOIDING DANGLING MODIFIERS

Modifying clauses and phrases can add variety and details to writing. Generally, modifiers should be close enough to the word they modify so that there is a clear relationship. When writers allow modifiers to slip away from the word they want to describe, or they provide no word for the modifier to describe, expression becomes confused (and sometimes unintentionally quite funny). Such modifiers are called dangling modifiers.

Procedure:

1. Explain that modifying clauses and phrases describe a word in a sentence. When it is unclear what a modifier describes, it is called a dangling modifier. This weakens writing by muddying the meaning of a sentence.

2. On the board or an overhead projector, offer these examples of dangling modifiers:

   Driving alone for the first time, the sputtering engine frightened her.

   Note that the modifying phrase "Driving alone for the first time" seems to imply that the engine was driving.

   While in the final mile of the race, her ankle twisted.

   The modifier "While in the final mile of the race" seems to modify ankle. It sounds like the ankle was in the final mile of the race. Although technically it was, that's not what the author intended to say.

   Magnificent and awe-inspiring, he wanted to reach the peak of the mountain.

   This construction sounds like the mountain climber was "magnificent and awe-inspiring" when the phrase in fact describes the peak.

3. Explain that to avoid dangling modifiers writers must make sure that modifying phrases and clauses clearly are linked to the words they are supposed to describe. Show students ways to correct the above examples:

   Driving alone for the first time, she was frightened by the sputtering engine.

   The opening phrase clearly modifies "she" in this construction.

   While in the final mile of the race, Kelly twisted her ankle.

   The opening clause modifies "Kelly."

   Because the peak of the mountain was magnificent and awe-inspiring, he wanted to reach it.

   He wanted to reach the magnificent and awe- inspiring peak of the mountain.

   In either revision for this sentence, it becomes obvious that "magnificent and awe-inspiring" modifies the mountain peak.

4. Mention that modifying clauses usually modify the word right next to them.

MINI-LESSON 62:
TENSES — CHOOSING THE PRESENT OR PAST

Before an author writes a piece, she must decide whether she will use the present or past tense. Although the past tense is far more common, there are times when your students will find the present tense more helpful in the communication of their ideas.

Procedure:

1. Explain that articles or stories can be written in the present or past tense.

2. Mention that the past tense is the more commonly used tense in stories or narratives, because most pieces are written about events that have already happened. Using the past tense, therefore, is logical. Offer these examples of the simple past tense on the board or an overhead projector:

   Sammy applied for the job.

   She was elected senior class president.

3. Discuss that the present tense, although rarely used in stories, is commonly used in essays, criticism, editorials, and how-to articles. It is used when the author wants to communicate a feeling that something is occurring right now. Use of the present tense can evoke a sense of immediacy, as if the reader, along with the author, is experiencing the events as they happen. Offer these examples:

   She plays clarinet in the state orchestra.

   First, attach the hinges to the door, and then set the door in the frame.

4. Emphasize that whatever tense an author selects, he or she should be consistent with it. Switching from past to present and then back to past is disruptive and confusing to readers.

MINI-LESSON 63:
*THE PAST PERFECT — SHOWING PREVIOUS PAST ACTION*_____

Most students handle simple past tense adequately. They are familiar with it because they use it in speaking. Showing previous past action, however, is troublesome for many students.

Procedure:

1. Explain that action that happens before some other past action needs to be designated in writing. The most common way of doing this is to use the past perfect tense. This verb form uses *had* and the past participle of the main verb. Offer these examples on the board or an overhead projector:

   After she had gone (not went) to school, she applied for the position of manager.

   Note that the action of going to school came before applying for the manager's position, and it is shown by the past perfect verb phrase "had gone."

   He had had good seasons, but this one was the best.

   Point out that "had had" is correct. (Many students assume it is wrong because of the repetition of "had.") It shows that he "had" good seasons in the past, before the one that "was the best."

   After she had made the plans, the vacation was canceled.

   Note that "had made" shows that the plans were made before the vacation was canceled.

2. Emphasize that the past perfect tense is often used to introduce flashbacks for stories. (See Mini-lesson 37.) Note that once the flashback is established, the past perfect is dropped in favor of the simple past. Overusing the past perfect can result in cumbersome, awkward writing.

MINI-LESSON 64:
DID OR DONE

Some students make the mistake of using "done" for the past tense of "do."

Procedure:

1. Explain that the past tense of "do" is "did." Some authors mistakenly write "done" instead. Although "done" is used as the past tense in some places in spoken language, it is not used in standard English. Offer this example on the board or an overhead projector:

   Incorrect
   They done the project at home.

   Correct
   They did the project at home.

2. Note that "done" always requires a helping verb, for example, *was done, has done, had done, will have done,* and so on. Offer these examples:

   The firefighters could not have done anything more.

   The job will be done on time.

3. Caution students to avoid using "done" as the past tense with singular nouns and pronouns. Offer this example:

   Incorrect
   Dan done all he could to find the missing ring.

   Correct
   Dan did all he could to find the missing ring.

MINI-LESSON 65:
*WRITING WITH SOUNDS THAT AREN'T WORDS*_____

Many authors, particularly students, use sound effects in their writing. To help ensure that they use such words correctly, you might offer this mini-lesson. It's usually fun.

Procedure:

1. Explain that sometimes authors use sound effects in their writing. Sound effects can heighten drama, add emphasis, or make dialogue seem more realistic.

2. Caution students not to overuse sound-effect words, because they can become distracting and undermine ideas. Moreover, used too often, they may make writing sound juvenile.

3. On the board or an overhead projector, offer these examples of sound-effect words with their meanings:

   > *ahh*—a pause, or an interjection that shows emotion
   > *arghhh*—agony or pain
   > *gasp*—a short, sharp intake of breath, usually during great emotion
   > *hmm*—a thoughtful pause
   > *mmm*—a sound of noncommitment
   > *oh*—an interjection that usually shows surprise or great emotion
   > *shh*—an urge to silence
   > *sigh*—a long exhalation of breath
   > *uhh*—hesitation
   > *uh-huh*—yes
   > *uh-oh*—oh no
   > *uh-uh*—no
   > *yeah or yeh*—yes
   > *yay*—a cheer

4. Note a caution on the use of "gasp" and "sigh." Occasionally, they are used with dialogue: "Look out!" gasped John, or "It's finally over," she sighed. In a technical sense, neither construction is correct. A person can't gasp or sigh words. A gasp is a short intake of breath. When one takes breath in, he or she can't speak. Speech is formulated by the exhalation of air over the vocal cords. When one sighs, he or she releases air but does not speak. If the person speaks, he or she is not sighing.

MINI-LESSON 66:
AVOIDING DOUBLE NEGATIVES

Double negatives are considered to be poor usage because they use two negative words when one is sufficient. There are several word combinations that result in double negatives.

Procedure:

1. Explain that double negatives are instances in which two negative words are used when one is needed. Negative words imply "no." Offer this example of a glaring double negative on the board or an overhead projector:

    We don't have no gym class today because of the assembly.

    Point out that "not" in *don't* and "no" are two negatives. In a strict reading, if you *don't* have *no* gym, you have gym. Thus, in many cases, double negatives cancel themselves out and offer the opposite meaning. Offer the corrected sentence:

    We don't have any gym class today because of the assembly.

2. Explain that several common usages result in double negatives. Words like *hardly, scarcely,* and *but* when combined with "not" often result in double negatives. Offer this example with the correction:

    You can't hardly tell the differences among the varieties of tomatoes.
    Corrected: You can hardly tell the differences among the varieties of tomatoes.

3. Emphasize that the best way to eliminate double negatives is to drop one of the negative words.

4. Note that, for fiction, having a character speak with double negatives is an excellent means of showing an "uneducated" character.

MINI-LESSON 67: ITALICS FOR TITLES AND NAMES

Italics are used to identify or designate certain titles and names. *In print, italicized words lean to the right, as this sentence shows.* When writing in longhand, or using a typewriter or printer that doesn't have italicizing capability, writers indicate italics by <u>underlining</u>. Students often confuse italics with quotation marks, especially for titles.

Procedure:

1. Explain that italics is a print style in which words lean to the right. Show students an example — if possible from one of their texts — or copy or project the top part of this page.

2. Write the following examples of the uses of italics on the board or an overhead projector:

   > (1) Titles of books
   > (2) Titles of magazines and newspapers
   > (3) Titles of movies
   > (4) Titles of plays
   > (5) Titles of operas
   > (6) Titles of paintings
   > (7) Names of planes
   > (8) Names of trains
   > (9) Names of ships
   > (10) Names of spacecraft

3. Note that when they can't use italics in their writing, students should use underlining. (When editors mark typewritten script for italicizing, they underline it.)

MINI-LESSON 68:
ITALICS FOR EMPHASIS

Italics are often used for emphasis. Since the use of italics in general is misunderstood by many students, a mini-lesson showing how italics can highlight words and ideas can be helpful.

Procedure:

1. Remind students that italics are indicated by words that are slanted to the right.

2. Explain that italics have two important uses. One is for designating titles (see Mini-lesson 67), and the other is for providing emphasis for words and ideas. Mention that quotation marks can also be used for emphasis and that writers choose how they highlight their work. Offer these examples on the board or an overhead projector:

   "Did you see *that*?" Carol said.

   Note how the use of italics for *that* indicates the word is to be emphasized.

   She read the final clue on the treasure map. *"Look below the hollow oak."*

   Note that the clue is italicized, which adds great emphasis.

3. Caution students not to overuse the techniques for emphasis. Too much italics, for example, calls attention to itself and undermines the words and ideas it is supposed to be highlighting.

MINI-LESSON 69:
USING QUOTATION MARKS FOR TITLES_____

Quotation marks have many uses in writing. One of these uses is to designate titles. (For the use of quotation marks with dialogue, see Mini-lesson 35, and for the use of quotation marks for emphasis, see Mini-lesson 70.)

Procedure:

1. Show quotation marks (" ") on the board or an overhead projector.

2. Explain that one of the uses of quotation marks is to identify the titles of stories, magazine articles, short poems, chapters in books, and episodes of TV shows. Offer these examples:

   "The Open Window" by H. H. Munro is an amusing short story.

   "Ozymandias" is a poem by Percy B. Shelley.

   "How to Travel with Your Pet" is an article that all pet owners who travel with their pets should read.

   Chapter 6, "Acing Your Tests," was the best part of the book, *Study for Success.*

   The TV show "I Love Lucy" remains popular today.

3. Note that the titles of books, movies, and plays are italicized. Offer these examples:

   Gone with the Wind is an excellent novel about the Civil War.

   The Terminator was a top-selling movie.

   Death of a Salesman is considered by many to be a classic American play.

MINI-LESSON 70:
USING QUOTATION MARKS FOR EMPHASIS

Along with other uses (such as setting off dialogue, quoting sources, and identifying titles), quotation marks can be used for emphasis. (For the use of quotation marks with dialogue, see Mini-lesson 35, and for the use of quotation marks for titles, see Mini-lesson 69.)

Procedure:

1. Explain that quotation marks can be used to emphasize words that an author uses in special ways. Offer this example on the board or an overhead projector:

   Tom is "energetic." He has trouble sitting still in one place very long.

   In this case, "energetic" was used to suggest politely that Tom is hyperactive. The author is drawing attention to a case of deliberate understating.

2. Point out that quotation marks can be used to emphasize the introduction of new or unfamiliar words. Offer this example:

   "Electronic mail" makes many businesses more efficient.

   Point out that in this case the quotation marks are used to highlight a new term that hasn't yet become a standard part of the language.

3. Mention that in most cases, quotation marks for emphasis can be replaced with italics or underlining (in lieu of italics).

MINI-LESSON 71:
USING PARENTHESES

Parentheses are used for including additional, but not essential, information to a sentence. Separating this information from the rest of the sentence makes the sentence easier to understand.

Procedure:

1. Show the parentheses signs (   ) on the board or an overhead projector.

2. Explain that parentheses are used to provide additional or incidental information to a sentence. Since this information is not as important as the rest of the material, it is separated from the rest of the sentence with parentheses. Offer these examples:

   Ernest Hemingway (1899-1961) is one of the best-known American authors.

   Note that since the years of his life are not essential information, they are put in parentheses.

   The inside of a computer (see Figure 3) has few moving parts.

   Mention that Figure 3 directs readers to a picture that supports the text. However, this information would disrupt the sentence if it were not in parentheses.

3. To check if they have used parentheses correctly, suggest that students ask themselves if the material they placed inside parentheses is needed by the sentence. If the answer is yes, parentheses should not be used. The exception might be in informal writing, as in the case of an authorial aside.

4. Explain that punctuation marks fall outside parentheses, unless they apply to the information inside. Offer these two examples:

   He couldn't go (not that he wanted to).

   John said (surprise!) that he didn't want to go.

MINI-LESSON 72:
USING THE DASH

Dashes should be used conservatively in writing. Too many make an author's style choppy. However, the dash can be used effectively as a dramatic pause.

Procedure:

1. Show students the dash (—) on the board or an overhead projector. On typewriters and word processors, the dash is made of two hyphens, with one space on either side.

2. Explain that the dash is used for a dramatic pause. It may set off information at the end of the sentence, or it may interrupt the sentence. Offer these examples:

   There was no way out of this — Lisa had to tell her parents the truth.

   She was convinced that she had been here before — she knew every detail of the ruins — but that was impossible.

3. Mention that dashes should be used only when necessary. Too many disrupt the flow of an author's style and make his or her writing rough.

MINI-LESSON 73:
*USING HYPHENS WITH COMPOUND WORDS AND NUMBERS*_____

Hyphens are used to form some compound words and the numbers from 21 to 99, or numbers that end with 21 through 99. Many students have trouble with, or ignore, the use of hyphens in such instances.

Procedure:

1. Explain that hyphens are used to form some compound words. Offer these examples on the board or an overhead projector:

   brother-in-law   all-round   good-looking
   able-bodied   well-to-do   life-size

2. Note that compound words can be tricky. Even dictionaries don't always agree as to which ones need hyphens. Students should consult a dictionary whenever they are uncertain whether to use a hyphen for compound words.

3. Point out that hyphens should always be used to join two or more words that form a single adjective before a noun. Offer these examples:

   fifteen-year-old girl   well-known author

4. Explain that hyphens are used with compound numbers from 21 to 99. Offer these examples:

   twenty-one   ninety-nine
   three hundred fifty-two

5. Mention that, usually, as a compound construction becomes part of the language, the hyphens disappear. The exceptions are when the result would be unwieldy, for example, "brotherinlaw" or "welltodo."

MINI-LESSON 74:
*USING HYPHENS FOR SEPARATING SYLLABLES*_____

Hyphens are used to divide words into syllables. Dividing words correctly causes confusion for some students.

Procedure:

1. Show a hyphen (-) on the board or on an overhead projector.

2. Explain that one of the most important uses of the hyphen is to divide words into syllables at the end of a line.

3. Note that breaking a word into one-letter syllables should be avoided. For example, *e-nough* should not be broken so that the "e" is on one line and "nough" is on the next. Also remind students that one-syllable words should never be broken.

4. Emphasize that students should consult a dictionary whenever they are unsure how a word should be broken into syllables.

5. Mention that students who use word processors usually don't have to worry about breaking words at the ends of lines. Most word-processing software features "wraparound." When a word runs past the margin, it is automatically brought to the next line. Students should not divide words if they have wraparound capability.

MINI-LESSON 75:
WRITING LISTS WITH COLONS AND COMMAS

Most of your students will know that commas are used with lists such as "apples, pears, and oranges" (or, depending on the style used, "apples, pears and oranges"). Some, however, will not be familiar with the use of colons to set off lists.

Procedure:

1. Explain that commas are used to separate items in a list. Colons are sometimes used to signal that a list is to follow. Offer these examples on the board or an overhead projector:

   With commas only
   They packed sandwiches, lemonade, and cookies for the picnic.

   With colon and commas
   The following students earned awards: Renée, Sheila, and Paulo.

2. Note that a colon should not be used after a verb or a preposition. Offer these examples:

   Incorrect
   The afternoon's major events are: tug-of-war, relay races, and softball.

   Note that the list follows the verb "are."

   Correct
   Here are the afternoon's major events: tug-of-war, relay races, and softball.

   Incorrect
   There were several sports he excelled in: football, basketball, baseball, and soccer.

   Here the list follows the preposition "in."

   Correct
   He excelled in several sports: football, basketball, baseball, and soccer.

MINI-LESSON 76:
SPELLING STRATEGY NUMBER ONE —
THE DICTIONARY

Spelling is a weakness for many students. While no spelling strategy and no amount of memorization will turn poor spellers into champions, the use of sound spelling strategies can reduce mistakes.

Procedure:

1. Explain to your students that correct spelling is important to their final copies. Pieces that are marred with spelling errors make a poor impression on readers. The errors stick out and detract from the author's ideas.

2. Mention that any piece that is submitted to a publication should be free of errors in spelling and mechanics. Pieces that possess spelling errors fail to make good impressions on editors.

3. Point out that every time a person misspells a word she reinforces in her mind the incorrect spelling. Thus, she is likely to misspell the word again. This is why some people keep misspelling the same words over and over again. Likewise, every time a word is spelled correctly, the correct spelling is reinforced.

4. Explain that students should consult a dictionary whenever they are unsure of the correct spelling of a word. Even professional authors rely on dictionaries for the proper spelling, pronunciation, meaning, and usage of words.

5. Be ready for the standard complaint of students. Inevitably, some will argue that they can't hope to find words in the dictionary if they don't know how to spell them. Explain that it is often easier than they think to find words in the dictionary. Usually, only a few letters are wrong in the misspelled word, often in the middle or near the end of the word. By looking up the first syllable, or first few letters, most words can be found. (There are some exceptions; for example, "psychology"; but these are rare.)

MINI-LESSON 77:
SPELLING STRATEGY NUMBER TWO —
*PROPER PRONUNCIATION*_____

Many students (and adults!) spell words incorrectly because they mispronounce them. They spell the word the way it sounds to them.

Procedure:

1. Explain that proper pronunciation is one of the keys to good spelling. People who don't say words correctly often have trouble spelling them. On the board or an overhead projector, offer these commonly mispronounced and misspelled words with their correct forms:

   idear — idea
   childern — children
   probly — probably
   tempature — temperature
   temperment — temperament
   disasterous — disastrous
   draw — drawer
   enviroment — environment
   stold — stole

2. Emphasize that students should listen carefully to the way words are spoken. If they are not sure of a pronunciation, they should consult a dictionary or ask a teacher or parent.

3. Suggest that students record these words on a page of their journals. Once a week they might share the words with a partner.

MINI-LESSON 78:
SPELLING STRATEGY NUMBER THREE —
SPELLING CONFUSIONS

Although not actually misspelled, students will often confuse words that have similar spellings. Homophones are a major source of such confusion.

Procedure:

1. Explain that homophones are words that have identical pronunciations but different meanings and spellings. Because of this, they are easy to misuse.

2. Note that in addition to homophones, other words close in pronunciation or spelling are easily confused.

3. Distribute copies of the accompanying "Spelling Confusions" or use an overhead projector and briefly review the pairs of words with your students. Ask students to supply additional words for this list.

4. Emphasize that the best way to avoid misusing homophones and other easily confused words is to become familiar with the different forms or consult a dictionary.

Spelling Confusions

Sometimes authors simply spell the wrong word. Following are homophones — words that sound alike but which have different meanings and spellings. Guard against making mistakes with them in your writing.

allowed, aloud	ate, eight
brake, break	capital, capitol
chord, cord	coarse, course
flea, flee	foul, fowl
know, no	lead, led
lessen, lesson	made, maid
not, knot	one, won
patience, patients	peace, piece
pray, prey	rain, reign, rein
right, rite, write	sew, so
soar, sore	some, sum
stake, steak	tail, tale
who's, whose	your, you're

Homophones aren't the only words that authors may confuse. Some words sound so much alike, or are spelled so similarly, that they often are used in place of each other.

advice, advise	bazaar, bizarre
breath, breathe	clothes, close
confidant, confident	country, county
device, devise	dual, duel
emigrate, immigrate	envelop, envelope
farther, further	later, latter
lightening, lightning	medal, metal
moral, morale	picture, pitcher
principal, principle	than, then
veracious, voracious	were, where

Note that there are many more words in both groups. Add more words on the lines below.

_____

_____

_____

_____

MINI-LESSON 79:
SPELLING STRATEGY NUMBER FOUR —
PERSONAL SPELLING LISTS

Maintaining personal spelling lists of difficult words is an easy way for students to improve their spelling.

Procedure:

1. Explain that keeping a personal list of hard-to-spell words is a helpful spelling strategy for many people. Every time the person misspells a word, he or she writes it in a notebook.

2. Suggest that students use notebooks with loose-leaf pages. They should enter the words alphabetically, skipping a few spaces between entries so that they can add more words later. (For students who have only a few troublesome words, suggest that they write them on a file card, which they can keep closeby while writing.)

3. Emphasize that students should check their list when they must use a word that gives them trouble. Using the word correctly will reinforce the right spelling. In time they will be using their lists less frequently.

MINI-LESSON 80:
AVOIDING SO MANY SO'S AND THEN'S

"So" and "then" are two of the most overused words in student writing. I've found that the major reason students rely on these words *so* much is that they don't realize the easy alternatives.

Procedure:

1. Explain that "so" and "then" are often overused. They frequently result in awkward constructions. On the board or an overhead projector, offer these examples:

    We didn't have our badges, so we couldn't get onto the beach.

    Angelo finished work, then he decided to call Ralph.

    Teresa saw the dark clouds gathering, so she knew it was going to rain.

2. Mention that the words "when" and "since" can often be used to revise sentences using "so" and "then." Offer these revisions of the previous examples:

    Since we didn't have our badges, we couldn't get onto the beach.

    When Angelo finished work, he called Ralph.

3. Note that sometimes "so" and "then" can be replaced with a conjunction such as *and, but,* or *or.* Offer this example:

    Teresa saw the dark clouds gathering, and she knew it was going to rain.

4. Caution students to avoid using "so" and "then" to start sentences. Offer these examples:

    So I went to work late.

    Then we got a ton of homework.

Note that "so" is unnecessary to the beginning of almost any sentence. While "then" can start a sentence, particularly when a time change is needed, it, too, should be used with care.

MINI-LESSON 81:
AFFECT AND EFFECT

These two words are regularly confused by students and adults. A mini-lesson on them can clarify their meanings and usage.

Procedure:

1. Explain that "affect" and "effect" are not synonyms, as many people believe they are. They cannot be used in place of each other.

2. Note that "affect" is usually a verb. It means to influence, sway, or impress. Offer these examples on the board or an overhead projector:

    The loss of the tennis match will affect Sabrina's confidence.

    The failure affected his mood for weeks.

3. Explain that "effect" is commonly used as a noun or a verb.

    a. As a noun, "effect" means the result of some action. Offer these examples:

    The effect of cooperation was an increase in production.

    What was the effect of the boycott?

    b. As a verb, "effect" means to accomplish something. Offer these examples:

    The new class president effected several important changes in school.

    The school administration will effect a new graduation policy by the spring.

4. Suggest that since these words are easily mixed up, students should consult dictionaries whenever they use them — until they become certain they are using "affect" and "effect" correctly.

MINI-LESSON 82:
ALL RIGHT AND (NOT) ALRIGHT

"All right" and "alright" are often found in print. I recall one article where the author used both forms within the space of a few paragraphs. Although many people use these words interchangeably, "all right" is the preferred usage.

Procedure:

1. Write the following two sentences on the board and ask students which one is correct:

   Everything is all right now.

   Everything is alright now.

2. Explain that although they likely will see "alright" in some of the material they read, it is not a preferred form in written English. It may be one day, as language is constantly evolving, but it isn't yet.

3. Point out that the preferred form is "all right." Offer these examples on the board or an overhead projector:

   The thunderstorm is done, and it is all right to go outside.

   "All right," said Les. "I'll see you at six."

   Is it all right to continue?

4. Suggest that students will find the correct form easier to remember by thinking of "all right" as two words. When they do they will most likely write "all right" and not "alright."

MINI-LESSON 83:
AMONG OR BETWEEN

In formal English "among" and "between" have distinct uses. You should share this distinction with your students.

Procedure:

1. Explain that although many people casually use the prepositions "among" and "between" in the same constructions, the words have distinct uses in formal English.

2. Point out that "among" is used with more than two people, ideas, or things. Offer these examples on the board or an overhead projector:

   The position of group leader alternates among five people.

   Ellen was uncomfortable among the other applicants.

3. Note that "between" is used when speaking of two people, ideas, or things. Offer these examples:

   What is the difference between History I and History I-A?

   The puppy ran between Chuck and Brian, and streaked across the yard.

   There are many differences between mammals and reptiles.

MINI-LESSON 84:
BAD AND BADLY

"Bad" and "badly" are different parts of speech and they have different roles in the sentence. Many students treat these words the same, however, which results in usage mistakes.

Procedure:

1. Explain that "bad" and "badly" have different functions in the sentence.

2. Note that "bad" is an adjective and can only modify nouns or pronouns. It is often used after the verb "to be" and verbs that refer to the senses such as *feel, look, seem, appear, smell, sound,* and *taste.* Offer these examples on the board or an overhead projector:

   He hated being called the bad apple. ("Bad" modifies the noun "apple.")

   After sweating all day, he smelled bad. ("Bad" modifies the pronoun "he.")

3. Mention that "badly" is an adverb. Most often it modifies verbs. It does not modify nouns or pronouns. Offer these examples:

   He played badly and struck out three times. ("Badly" modifies the verb "played.")

   Too many people drive badly in this town. ("Badly" modifies "drive.")

MINI-LESSON 85:
AVOIDING "COULD OF" AND SIMILAR CONSTRUCTIONS⎯⎯⎯⎯⎯⎯

How many times have you heard your students say something like, "I could of done that"? You probably see that phrase and others like it in their writing just as often.

Procedure:

1. Explain that phrases like "could of" (which the authors use to mean "could've") easily slip into writing because they are used in everyday speech. However, such phrases are careless expressions. Instead of "could of", for instance, the author means "could have." Offer these other examples of such phrases on the board or an overhead projector:

might of	must of
couldn't of	should of
shouldn't of	mustn't of

2. Point out that in all the above phrases, "of" should be replaced with "have." Offer these examples of sentences with corrections:

   Incorrect
   She could of asked him why.

   Correct
   She could have asked him why.

   Incorrect
   He shouldn't of done that.

   Correct
   He shouldn't have done that.

   Incorrect
   Rachelle must of spent $500.00 on school clothes.

   Correct
   Rachelle must have spent $500.00 on school clothes.

3. Emphasize that phrases such as "could of" are examples of poor writing. They should always be revised, replacing the "of" with "have."

MINI-LESSON 86:
FARTHER AND FURTHER

Few students are aware of the different uses of "farther" and "further." Teaching them such fine points of writing will help them to gain an appreciation for the depth and fine shadings of English.

Procedure:

1. Explain that "farther" and "further" have different meanings.

2. Note that "farther" is concerned with physical distances. Offer these examples on the board or an overhead projector:

   Randy hiked farther than he ever had.

   How much farther is the next rest area?

   The sun is much farther from the Earth than the moon is.

3. Point out that "further" is concerned with degree or quantity. It is often used to mean "more" or "in addition." Offer these examples on the board or an overhead projector:

   A further reason to leave early was to avoid rush-hour traffic.

   "Further," said Professor Stone, "economics was a major factor of the Civil War."

   Further investigation revealed that she had driven farther than she had claimed.

4. Suggest this easy way to remember when to use "farther" or "further."

   a. Distance requires "farther"; an example is: a mile farther.

   b. Quantity, degree, or reasons require "further."

MINI-LESSON 87:
FEWER OR LESS

The correct use of "fewer" or "less" is overlooked by many writers. These two words represent one of the finer points of written language that your students should recognize.

Procedure:

1. Explain that "fewer" and "less" have different uses in the sentence.
2. Point out that "fewer" refers to the amount of things you can count and is used before plural nouns. Offer these examples on the board or an overhead projector:

   Fewer spectators watched the game yesterday.

   Note that "spectators" is a plural noun and that "fewer" refers to the number of spectators.

   This monorail seats fewer people than the last one did.

   Note that "fewer" refers to the number of people.

3. Explain that "less" refers to degree or size or the amount of something that can't be counted such as hair or sand and is used with singular nouns. Offer this example:

   With the camping equipment loaded, the car has less space for passengers.

   Note that "less" refers to the amount of space in the car. Also note that "space" is a singular noun.

   They had less trouble at last night's dance.

   Note that "less" refers to the degree of trouble. "Trouble" is a singular noun.

   There is less sand at this end of the beach.

   Note that "less" refers to the amount of sand, which can't be counted.

MINI-LESSON 88:
GOOD AND WELL

"Good" and "well" are often misused. Understanding their functions in the sentence can help students avoid mistakes with these two words.

Procedure:

1. Ask your students to raise their hands if they are sure how "good" and "well" are used in sentences. It is unlikely that you'll see many hands up.

2. Explain that "good" is always an adjective. It modifies nouns or pronouns. Like "bad" it often follows the verb "to be" or verbs that describe the senses. Offer these examples on the board or an overhead projector:

    It had been a good day. ("Good" modifies "day.")

    He looked good in his new suit. ("Good" modifies "he.")

3. Point out that "well" may be used either as an adjective or an adverb.

    a. Note that as an adjective, "well" is often used to refer to health. Offer this example:

    Lance feels well.

    b. Note that as an adjective, "well" also may refer to a satisfactory condition. Offer this example:

    After the initial problem was corrected, everything was well.

    c. Note that as an adverb, "well" means to do something capably. Offer this example:

    Mira performed well in the play.

4. Caution students to consult style books or their language texts regularly until they gain a thorough understanding of "good" and "well."

MINI-LESSON 89:
IN AND INTO

Few students have any inkling of the different uses of "in" and "into." Still, the distinction is an example of one of the fine points of writing that you should share with them.

Procedure:

1. Explain that "in" and "into" have slightly different uses.
2. Note that "in" means within or being "inside." Offer these examples on the board or an overhead projector:

   They waited in the hospital's lounge. (They were already "inside," thus "in" is used.)

   The old furniture is stored in the garage. (The furniture is already "within" the garage, and the construction requires "in.")

3. Explain that "into" implies movement to the inside. Offer these examples:

   They walked into the house. (The movement is from outside to inside.)

   After making her wish, Vera tossed the coin into the wishing well. (The coin moves from outside the well to inside the well.)

4. Suggest this easy way to remember the difference between "in" and "into."
   a. "In" means *already* inside.
   b. "Into" means moving to the inside.

MINI-LESSON 90:
IT'S AND ITS

"It's" and "its" are two of the most commonly confused pronouns. Mistakes in their usage even slip into printed material, and it's not surprising that students mix-up the two forms.

Procedure:

1. Explain that to use the pronouns "it's" and "its" correctly, authors must understand the meanings of the two words.

2. Point out that "it's" is a contraction for "it is." On the board or an overhead projector, offer this example:

    It's going to rain.
    It is going to rain.

    Note that the contraction takes the place of "it is" and requires the apostrophe.

3. Emphasize that "its" is the possessive form of the pronoun "it." An apostrophe *is not* used which is an exception to the customary rules of possession. Offer this example:

    The valley was a lonely place, but its beauty was breathtaking.

    Note that "its" refers to valley. The valley's beauty was breathtaking.

4. Tell students that by breaking apart the contraction for "it's," they will be able to see if they are using the correct form.

    It's a nice day for a picnic.
    It is a nice day for a picnic. (*correct*)

    Now offer this example:

    It's fur is brown and tan.
    It is fur is brown and tan. (*incorrect*)

    In this sentence, "its" is the correct form.

    Its fur is brown and tan.

MINI-LESSON 91:
THERE, THEIR, AND THEY'RE

These three words seem to be bewildering for some students, as well as for some adults. Even after offering a mini-lesson concerning them, you will still need to review their usage during writing conferences.

Procedure:

1. Explain that writers must understand the differences among "there," "their," and "they're."

2. Point out the various meanings of "there" and offer examples on the board or an overhead projector:

    a. "There" means in that place.
       The coat rack is over there.

    b. "There" can start sentences when linked with the verb "to be."
       There is a parking lot at the hotel.

    c. "There" can be used as an interjection.
       There! I've finally finished.

3. Emphasize that "their" is a possessive pronoun. Offer this example:

    They left their bikes behind the school.

    Note that "their" is plural and must be linked to plural nouns or pronouns. Offer this example:

    Incorrect
    Someone left their gloves on the table.

    Correct
    Someone left his or her gloves on the table.

    They left their gloves on the table.

    Note that "Someone" is singular and requires a singular pronoun, either "his" or "her." Changing "Someone" to "They" agrees with "their."

4. Explain that "they're" is a contraction for "they are." Offer this example:

    They're planning to leave by six.

    Note that to ensure they are using "they're" correctly, students should break the contraction and substitute "they are" in the sentence.

    They are planning to leave by six.

MINI-LESSON 92:
WHO'S OR WHOSE

"Who's" and "whose" are the culprits of plenty of mistakes. A good mini-lesson can help students see and remember the differences between these two words.

Procedure:

1. Explain that "who's" and "whose" do not mean the same thing.

2. Note that "who's" is a contraction for "who is" or "who has." Offer these examples on the board or an overhead projector:

   > Who's the driver of that car?
   > (Who is the driver of that car?)

   > Who's left the milk on the table?
   > (Who has left the milk on the table?)

3. Emphasize that "whose" is a possessive pronoun that shows ownership. Offer these examples:

   > Whose car is that?
   > Whose books are they?

   Note that in each example "whose" indicates ownership of the car or the books.

4. Suggest that breaking the contraction "who's" can help with usage. Offer this example:

   > Whose hat is on the rack?
   > Who's hat is on the rack?

   Ask how many students, by a show of hands, believe the first sentence is correct. Now ask how many believe the second one is correct. Show them that breaking the contraction makes it easy to see the correct form.

   > Who is hat is on the rack?

   Note that "whose" is the correct word in this sentence.

MINI-LESSON 93:
YOUR AND YOU'RE _____

Like other pronouns and contractions that are homophones, "your" and "you're" are regularly substituted for each other.

Procedure:

1. Explain that "your" and "you're" are homophones. Although they sound the same, they have different spellings and meanings.

2. Point out that "your" is a possessive pronoun. Offer these examples on the board or an overhead projector:

   Where is your jacket?

   Your books are on the table.

   Remember to lock your car doors.

3. Note that "you're" is a contraction for "you are." Offer these examples:

   You're taking Flight 209.
   (You are taking Flight 209.)

   Be careful where you're going.
   (Be careful where you are going.)

4. Suggest that breaking the contraction can help ensure correct usage. Offer this example:

   Your an excellent typist.

   Ask how many students, by a show of hands, believe the sentence is correct. Substitute the contraction "you're"; then break it.

   You're an excellent typist.
   You are an excellent typist.

   Emphasize the correct form.

MINI-LESSON 94:
*LAY AND LIE*_____

It is the rare person who *doesn't*, at least on occasion, confuse "lay" and "lie."

Procedure:

1. Explain that "lay" and "lie" are two verbs that are constantly being confused.

2. Note that "lay" means to put something down or to place something. Its principal parts are *lay, laid,* (have) *laid,* and *laying.* Offer these examples on the board or an overhead projector:

   Reece laid the tools down on the table.

   "Lay the seat covers there," said Martin.

   Where did I lay my books?

   Note that in each case, "put" can replace "lay."

3. Point out that "lie" means to rest or recline. (Note that it is not "lying" as in prevaricating.) Its principal parts are *lie, lay,* (have) *lain,* and *lying.* Point out that its past tense *lay* should not be confused with the verb "lay" (meaning to put). Offer these examples:

   She likes to lie down after work.

   He lay on the couch and napped for an hour.

   Jules is lying in the hammock.

   Alisha isn't feeling well; she has lain in bed all afternoon.

4. Suggest that the best way to use these verbs correctly is to memorize their parts. Offer these two tips as well:

   When a verb is needed to express the action of reclining, "lie" should be used.

   When a verb is needed to express the action of putting something down, "lay" should be used.

MINI-LESSON 95:
LOSE OR LOOSE

While most of your students will know the meanings of these two words, many will be unsure of the spellings and will use them incorrectly.

Procedure:

1. Explain that "lose" and "loose" have different pronunciations and meanings.

2. Mention that "lose" means to experience a loss. Offer these example sentences on the board or an overhead projector:

   When did you lose your keys?

   Brad will lose the game if he doesn't concentrate.

   Note that the past tense of "lose" is "lost." Offer this example:

   Brianne lost her purse.

3. Note that "loose" means unconnected or not close together. Offer these examples:

   The animals ran loose in the park.

   The hinge on the door was loose.

4. Suggest that students remember when to use "lose" by recalling this example:

   I hate to *lose* money. ("Lose" implies a loss of some kind.)

   Note that understanding when to use "lose" will help them to know when to use "loose."

MINI-LESSON 96:
USING "OF" RATHER THAN "OFF OF" _____

"Off of" is frequently used when "off" is sufficient. It is a type of overwriting of which students should be aware.

Procedure:

1. Explain that many people use the phrase "off of" when they should simply use "off." Offer these examples on the board or an overhead projector:

   Will moved the box off of the table.
   Revised: Will moved the box off the table.

   The squirrel jumped off of the tree branch.
   Revised: The squirrel jumped off the tree branch.

2. Note that sometimes the phrase "off from" is used. This, too, should be avoided because "off" is sufficient. Offer this example:

   Shel climbed off from the ledge.
   Revised: Shel climbed off the ledge.

MINI-LESSON 97:
SIT AND SET

Since *sit* and *set* are commonly misused in speaking, it is easy to understand why they are regularly interchanged in writing. Even some professional authors have trouble distinguishing between the two.

Procedure:

1. Explain that *sit* and *set* are two commonly misused words. Offer these definitions:
   a. Sit means to be in an upright position; "sitting" in a chair.
   b. Set means to place or put something somewhere.
2. Offer examples on the board or an overhead projector:

   Sit
   > Julio is sitting in the third row.
   > He sat through a two-hour lecture.

   Set
   > Artie set the vase on the windowsill.
   > Bea is setting the table now.

3. Suggest that students remember the differences between the two words in this way:

   > After I *set* the table, I *sat* down and ate.

Extension:

To give students more help with *sit* and *set*, offer the forms of the verbs on the board or an overhead projector:

Infinitive	Past	Present Participle	Past Participle
sit	sat	is sitting	(have) sat
set	set	is setting	(have) set

Point out that *set* has no spelling change.

MINI-LESSON 98:
THAN OR THEN

It seems that "than" and "then" are forever being confused. Only a clear understanding of their meanings and usage can prevent mistakes.

Procedure:

1. Emphasize that to use "than" and "then" correctly writers must understand their meanings.

2. Note that "than" is a conjunction, a word that joins parts of a sentence, especially before a comparison. Offer these examples on the board or an overhead projector:

   Mary is taller than Rose.

   Note that "than" connects "Rose" with "Mary is taller . . ."

   The science test was harder than the math test.

   Here "than" connects the first part of the sentence with the second.

3. Explain that "then" is usually an adverb. It means at that time. Its purpose in a sentence is to denote time or a relationship regarding time. Offer these examples:

   First they went skating. Then they built a snow sculpture.

   Kara finished the report at nine, and then relaxed by watching a movie.

4. Suggest that your students can remember the difference between "than" and "then" by recalling these sentences:

   AA is greater than A. ("A" is for "than.")

   Remind them that "than" connects parts of a sentence.

   Do E first, then go on. ("E" is for "then.")

   Remind them that "then" denotes time or a sequence.

MINI-LESSON 99:
TO, TOO, OR TWO

Few students at one time or another have trouble using "to," "too," or "two" correctly. A mini-lesson on the usage of these words is necessary in most writing workshops.

Procedure:

1. Explain that "to," "too," and "two" are often misused.
2. Point out that "to" is a preposition or part of an infinitive verb. Offer these examples on the board or an overhead projector:

   Carla went to Europe for three weeks. ("To" is a preposition.)

   After his car broke down, Tim had to walk three miles to the nearest phone. ("To" is part of the infinitive "to walk.")

3. Note that "too" is an adverb. It usually means *an excessive amount* or *also*. Offer these examples:

   It was raining too hard to walk home. ("Too hard" means an excessive amount.)

   Harold wanted to go, too. ("Too" means also.)

   Note that, when used to mean also, "too" is usually set off with commas.

   We, too, missed our plane.
   (We, also, missed our plane.)

4. Emphasize that "two" is the number 2. Offer this example:

   They arrived at two o'clock.

   Stan had to wait two hours for his train.

5. Emphasize that substituting "to," "too," and "two" for each other is easy. Too easy. To avoid misusing them, authors must understand their meanings and proofread their work carefully.

MINI-LESSON 100:
WHO OR WHOM?

The correct use of "who" or "whom" is an ongoing dilemma for many writers. For many the confusion begins in elementary school and continues long afterward. By presenting a mini-lesson on the topic, and reviewing the proper uses of these words during writer's conferences, you will help your students to use them correctly in their writing.

Procedure:

1. Explain that authors must be careful to use "who" and "whom" correctly. These two words are often misused.

2. Point out that "who" and "whom" are pronouns. The easiest way to remember the correct usage is to substitute "he" or "she" for "who" and "him" or "her" for "whom." Offer these examples on the board or an overhead projector:

   "Who"
   > Who was at the door?
   > He (or she) was at the door.

   Note that questions are rewritten as statements when "he" or "she" is substituted. Also point out that "He" fits the construction, therefore "who" is correct. Try this next example:

   > Whom lost his keys?
   > Him lost his keys.

   Note that substituting "Him" in this sentence is not correct. It doesn't sound right. Instead of "whom," "who" is needed.

   "Whom"
   > Whom did Josie see?
   > Josie saw him (or her).

   Note that substituting "he" for "him" will sound awkward. (Also note the change to simple past tense.)

   > Josie saw he.

   Since "him" is the proper substitute, "whom" is the correct pronoun.

3. Explain that "whom" often follows prepositions such as "to," "for," "with," or "from." Offer these examples:

   > To whom was the letter sent?
   > With whom did you drive to Texas?

4. Emphasize that memorizing the correct uses of "who" and "whom" is the best way to ensure using these words correctly.

5. Remind students that substituting "he" or "she" for "who" and "him" or "her" for "whom" is a good way to self-test the correct usage of these words.

Books and Resources for Teachers of Writing

Atwell, Nancie. *In the Middle: Writing, Reading, and Learning with Adolescents.* Montclair, NJ: Boynton/Cook, 1987.

Calkins, Lucy. *The Art of Teaching Writing.* Portsmouth, NH: Heinemann, 1986.

Elbow, Peter. *Writing with Power: Techniques for Mastering the Writing Process.* New York: Oxford University Press, 1981.

Emig, Janet. *The Web of Meaning.* Montclair, NJ: Boynton/Cook, 1982.

Graves, Donald H. *Children Want to Write.* Portsmouth, NH: Heinemann, 1982.

Graves, Donald H. *Writing: Teachers and Children at Work.* Portsmouth, NH: Heinemann, 1983.

Henderson, Kathy. *Market Guide for Young Authors.* Crozet, VA: Betterway Publications, Inc., 1990.

Hillerich, Robert. *Teaching Children to Write, K-8.* Englewood Cliffs, NJ: Prentice Hall, 1985.

Johnson, Pauline. *Creative Bookbinding.* Seattle and London: University of Washington Press, 1973.

Kissling, Mark (ed.). *Writer's Market.* Cincinatti, OH: F & W Publications, 1993.

Koch, Kenneth. *Rose, Where Did You Get that Red?* New York: Random House, 1973.

Koch, Kenneth. *Wishes, Lies, and Dreams: Teaching Children to Write Poetry.* New York: Harper and Row, 1970.

Murray, Donald M. *Learning by Teaching: Selected Articles on Writing and Teaching.* Montclair, NJ: Boynton/Cook, 1982.

Muschla, Gary Robert. *The Writing Teacher's Book of Lists*. Englewood Cliffs, NJ: Prentice Hall, 1991.

Muschla, Gary Robert. *Writing Resource Activities Kit: Ready-to-Use Worksheets and Enrichment Lessons for Grades 4-9*. West Nyack, NY: The Center for Applied Research in Education, 1989.

Newkirk, Thomas, and Nancie Atwell (eds.). *Understanding Writing: Ways of Observing, Learning, and Teaching*. Portsmouth, NH: Heinemann, 1988.

Padgett, Ron (ed.). *The Teachers and Writers Handbook of Poetic Forms*. New York: Teachers and Writers Collaborative, 1987.

Romano, Tom. *Clearing the Way: Working with Teenage Writers*. Portsmouth, NH: Heinemann, 1987.

Smith, Frank. *Writing and the Writer*. Hillsdale, NJ: Lawrence Erlbaum Associates, 1982.

Tchudi, Stephen N., and Susan J. Tchudi. *The English/Language Arts Handbook: Classroom Strategies for Teachers*. Portsmouth, NH: Heinemann, 1991.

Weiss, Harvey. *How to Make Your Own Books*. New York: Thomas Y. Crowell Company, 1974.

Zemelman, Steven, and Harvey Daniels. *A Community of Writers: Teaching Writing in the Junior and Senior High School*. Portsmouth, NH: Heinemann, 1988.

Zinsser, William. *On Writing Well*. New York: Harper and Row, 1985.

DATE DUE

Demco, Inc. 38-293